GRANT FUHR

THE STORY OF A HOCKEY LEGEND

WITH BRUCE DOWBIGGIN

RANDOM HOUSE CANADA

PUBLISHED BY RANDOM HOUSE CANADA

www.randomhouse.ca

LIBRARY AND ARCHIVES CANADA CATALOGUING IN PUBLICATION

Fuhr, Grant, 1962–, author
Grant Fuhr : the story of a hockey legend / Grant Fuhr with Bruce
Dowbiggen.

Includes bibliographical references and index.
Issued in print and electronic formats.
ISBN 978-0-307-36281-0
eBook ISBN 978-0-307-36283-4

1. Fuhr, Grant, 1962–. 2. Hockey goalkeepers—Canada—Biography. 3. Hockey
players—Canada—Biography. 4. Black Canadian hockey players—Biography. I.
Dowbiggin, Bruce, author II. Title.

GV848.5.F87A3 2014   796.962092   C2014-902984-5

Book design by CS Richardson
Cover image: © David E. Klutho / Sports Illustrated / Getty Images
Interior goalie silhouette: © Daniel Schweinert / Shutterstock.com

Printed and bound in the United States of America

2 4 6 8 9 7 5 3 1

CONTENTS

FOREWORD

Around 2001, my family had new neighbours living on our street in the Signal Hill area of Calgary. They were from Texas, and everything about winter was a revelation for them. The snow. The cold. The clothing. At the time they loved it. They also loved the quiet family across the street. "They're so nice," Colleen Moreland would say in her Texas drawl. "I'm not sure what he does, but he seems like a very nice man. Quiet but nice."

The quiet man she referred to just happened to be one of the greatest hockey goalies ever, Grant Fuhr. No Canadian could have missed the face, but my neighbour was blissfully unaware. I told her, imagine living across the street in Texas from Roger Clemens or Tony Dorsett. *That's* the status of Grant Fuhr in Canada's hockey hierarchy. Plus, he was the first black star in the game. Almost everywhere he goes in Canada he is immediately recognized by fans. She smiled apologetically and said, "I didn't know that. That's wonderful."

Grant *was* wonderful on the ice, but the unsuspecting acceptance of a neighbour was more comfortable for a man who preferred to be judged on his play rather than the colour of his skin
or the friends he kept. Grant had pursued hockey, and he got fame
in return. It was not always a great bargain living his life in the
eye of the media and fans. In retirement, Grant prefers the quiet
of the golf course to the throngs of people who want to shake his
hand. Like his parents, he's unimpressed with fame for its own
sake, and now prefers the anonymity of his current life and family.
He's earned that comfort. He sees his life as a learning example for
his four kids and for others who follow his exploits. It's an amazing tale of an adopted child of mixed race who emerged from a
small town in northern Alberta to become a household name in
Canada and around the hockey world. The saga of a star who
conquered hockey and his own problems with honesty and a
self-effacing smile. If you told people how it happened they
wouldn't believe you.

Here is the plain truth.

INTRODUCTION

On one glorious night, Toronto played host to a meeting of hockey royalty from the days of the NHL's last great dynasty—the Edmonton Oilers of 1984–90. Stars such as Wayne Gretzky, Kevin Lowe, Glen Sather and Paul Coffey filled the Great Hall of the Hockey Hall of Fame, while many teammates from the day were watching via the television broadcast. Coffey, the celebrated defenceman, sat just a few rows away from the podium where his former goalie Grant Fuhr now stood nervously in a tuxedo. One observer joked that this seat was probably closer than Coffey ever got to Fuhr on the ice during his legendary days rushing up to the other zone with the Edmonton Oilers. Like the best jokes, the jibe about the freewheeling Coffey had just enough truth to drive home the point. In his days as the Oilers' goalie, Grant was often a solo act, left to defend the home net while his prolific teammates swarmed the opposing end in search of goals, goals and more goals. The isolation—this abandonment by teammates—might have broken many other goalies. It's not hyperbole to say, as Ken Dryden once did, that goaltending is "grim, humorless, largely uncreative, getting little physical pleasure in return."

But Grant Fuhr never took it personally. With a characteristic shrug of the shoulders he'd just handle the opposing shooters all by himself. And on most nights during Edmonton's run of five Stanley Cups in seven years that's exactly what happened. No muss, no fuss. "It was well within his right to stand up and say, 'Come on guys, we're giving up five, six, seven breakaways per game,'" says teammate Marty McSorley. "He had every right to stand up in the dressing room and go, "C'mon guys,' but he never did. Not a peep of complaint."

For 17 NHL seasons, Grant defied the odds. And now, on this day, the Hall of Fame beckoned. As he nervously looked out over the assembled crowd to deliver his induction acceptance speech, the audience might have been forgiven for wondering where Fuhr might start. There was, after all, no easy way to sum him up, to describe his career. No. 31 was the culmination of the many streams flowing through his life and career. Starting out as an 18-day-old adoptee of mixed race in Spruce Grove, Alberta, with the most challenging of prospects, Fuhr authored a remarkable story of talent, resilience and a comeback from personal demons that almost ruined him and his career. Overcoming injuries in his mid-30s, he produced a triumphant second act in St. Louis long after the hockey "experts" thought he was finished.

Perhaps not surprisingly, he started his talk with the pioneer. The first superstar of colour in the NHL, Fuhr was a low-key model for racial equality in hockey, a worthy successor to pioneer Willie O'Ree, who broke the NHL's colour barrier in 1958. "I'd like to thank Willie O'Ree," Grant announced as O'Ree himself looked on from the crowd. "It's an extra-special honour to be the first man of colour in the Hockey Hall of Fame. It just shows that hockey is such a diverse sport that anyone can be successful in it. I'm proud of that, and I thank Willie for that."

To most of those gathered in the Great Hall, Grant was synonymous with the Oilers dynasty. It was hard to separate the kid who'd grown up in the Edmonton bedroom community of Spruce Grove from the city and that wonderful team. "I see Paul here, Wayne, Kevin [Lowe] . . . we had a huge family. It was all a team. More than a team it was a family. That said the most of it, and that's why we were successful."

Grant thanked one of the earliest Oilers for helping to launch his story. Ron Low took a teenaged goalie prospect fresh from the Victoria Cougars and taught him about life in the NHL. "He was my partner in my first year and a big part of where I am. For an 18-year-old goalie it takes a lot to get comfortable in the NHL, and Ronnie was a huge part of that. He was instrumental in that."

Grant also recalled two "special" relationships: one with the man who'd drafted him into the NHL, Oilers coach and general manager Glen Sather, and one with former Oilers and Buffalo Sabres coach John Muckler. "Glen and I probably had a little more special relationship than most coaches would want. I seemed to find a lot of time in his office. Some good, some bad. John Muckler, I seemed to spend a lot of time in that office too."

Mike Keenan, Grant's coach with Team Canada in the 1987 Canada Cup, revived the goalie's career late in his playing days, in St. Louis. "Lot of things have been said about him," Grant noted about Keenan. "His style's a little bit different, but he gave me a fabulous opportunity. It was a time in my career where you're thinking about quitting, and he gave me that opportunity to play. And I played a lot. He let me play every night. As a goalie that's what you want: the opportunity to play every night. And he gave me that."

It was also in St. Louis that Grant's unique approach to conditioning was changed for good by legendary Olympic coach Bobby

Kersee. "At one point I thought I was a good athlete," Fuhr said. "I was athletically good, but not a good athlete. Through Bobby, I found out what it was like to be a good athlete. I know Glen had pushed me to do that. Muck and I had a few conversations over that. I spent a lot of time riding a bike in Buffalo with one of our assistant coaches, John Tortorella. I might have been the only guy who rode every day and gained two pounds while the coach lost eight."

Finally, when conditioning was not enough, Grant's knees and shoulders were repaired by team doctors—extending his career to a remarkable 17 years at the top of the world's greatest hockey league. "They played a special part in my career," he said. "I spent a lot of time being put back together again. This body seems to have broken down a few times, and got written off a few times. But the doctors put me back together again."

Looking into the crowd, Grant could see his longtime friends and his four children, including son Robert (RJ)—wearing a suit for one of the few times in his life. "Kendyl, Rochelle, son RJ, daughter Janine: they make the big sacrifice. You get traded; you don't see the packing, you don't see the moving. Somehow it happens. We don't see that; we're pretty much married to the game of hockey. First and foremost, that's probably our wife—the game of hockey—and they take a back seat to that. I thank them for that.

"My friends have been there through thick and thin. I've had a different road than most people to get here. Most of it good, some not so good. A little bumpy along the way. But they've always been there. You have to have that love and support.

"In closing, it's the greatest game in the world, I'm happy to be part of it and I'm more happy to get back to it. It's special. Thank you."

To understand just how special requires a voyage through the singular games and moments of a remarkable life lived in full view.

GAME 1

Sports fans can be forgiven for failing to note the NHL debut of a wiry 19-year-old named Grant Fuhr against the Winnipeg Jets in the fourth game of the Edmonton Oilers' 1981–82 season. That same autumn day, Ray Burris of the Montreal Expos had out-duelled Fernando Valenzuela of the Los Angeles Dodgers 3–1 at Dodger Stadium—the first-ever League Championship Series win for a Canadian Major League Baseball team. Edmonton sports fans were also buzzing over the hometown Eskimos after their 24–6 win over the Ottawa Rough Riders pushed the defending Grey Cup champs to a 12–1–1 record in the Canadian Football League. In the NFL, Lawrence Taylor of the New York Giants was terrorizing quarterbacks just a month into his rookie season.

These were still the days before every game in a team's schedule was broadcast, before all-sports TV networks blanketed the medium with Top-10 lists and highlights from across the continent. What attention Grant's debut garnered came only from the local print and TV newscasts. No wonder there was less than a full house that night at Northlands Coliseum for what, in the end, would be an historic debut.

Besides, who was this junior kid, anyhow? Wasn't Andy Moog, the hero of the Oilers' dramatic sweep over Montreal in the 1981 playoffs, still the starter? Sure, Moog had stumbled, surrendering 10 goals while splitting his first two starts of the season. And Ron Low, on hand to be the reliable backup, had won 7–4 over the Los Angeles Kings just four nights before. There's that old expression—the one that says if an NHL team has two starting goalies then they've got none. And now the Oilers had *three* netminders? NHL teams can't carry three goalies: what was Oilers general manager (and coach) Glen "Slats" Sather thinking? Okay, maybe the Jets were a weak sister—brought in with the Oilers from the World Hockey Association and dead last at the end of the 1980–81 season—but this was no time for experimenting, not after the Oilers had proved themselves playoff worthy earlier in the year. Right?

If it was any consolation to the baffled 17,430 in attendance at Northlands Coliseum, Fuhr himself hadn't expected to be standing between the pipes against the Jets either. As he gazed down the ice at Winnipeg's rookie phenom, Dale Hawerchuk, his nemesis from the previous spring's Memorial Cup in the CHL, Grant had to be wondering what a teenager from Spruce Grove was suddenly doing in the uniform of his home team.

Grant:

I never even thought that I could stay in Edmonton my first year, because with Andy, the Oilers had won. The city was in love with him. Andy had played unbelievably against Montreal, and in those days it was unusual that they should beat Montreal, with Guy Lafleur and Larry Robinson and Serge Savard. We've also got Ronny Low there at the time and Gary Edwards. There were four or five guys that had NHL experience, besides Andy. I never even thought about making it the first camp. You keep waiting and waiting, thinking okay . . . you're watching all these other guys getting sent back down to the junior team—getting sent home. You figure at some point, you're going to get that call. So then I get the call up to the office and I go, "Okay. This must be it." When I get there Slats looks at me and says, "I think you should find a place to live here in Edmonton." The call never came.

All rookies experience some form of terror or nerves in their initial NHL game. But this first start was uncharted territory. Before Grant's introduction to the NHL, just a handful of teen-agers had donned the goalie pads in a league game before their 20th birthday. Player shortages during the Second World War had led the Detroit Red Wings to call up Harry Lumley (by no coincidence nicknamed "Apple Cheeks") at the tender age of 17. But Lumley was an exception in a time where there were just six starting jobs in the NHL, all of them dominated by veterans like Terry Sawchuk, Johnny Bower and Gump Worsley. And lack of opportunity wasn't the only factor working against teenaged hopefuls. When the NHL amateur draft was universalized in 1969, players weren't even eligible until the year of their 20th birthday. It wasn't until the World Hockey Association emerged in 1972 that teenaged players again got a chance to play in the pros. By 1981, 18- and 19-year-olds were finally eligible to play in the NHL, after threats of court challenges forced the league to match the WHA rules on eligibility. A few years earlier, Grant would have been looking at two more years of junior-level play, waiting impatiently for his chance to suit up with the big guys. Instead, he found himself starting for the Edmonton Oilers at the age of 19 years, 16 days.

But as Wayne Gretzky got set to take the opening faceoff for the Oilers that fine fall evening, Grant's youth took a backseat to something else that set the young goalie apart: he was the first black goalie to start an NHL game in the league's 64-year history.

———

In 1962, Bob and Betty Fuhr had reluctantly given up on the idea of having children themselves, and put their names in with various Alberta government agencies, signalling their desire to adopt. In the days before in-vitro fertilization and surrogate parenting, this was the common way to have a family when nature denied you one. For better or worse, there were still ample lists of children for adoption in that era, and in the Canada before cultural diversity, families wishing to adopt a child of their same culture or religion had a reasonable hope of doing so. Trans-racial adoptions were almost non-existent in North America until the 1950s, as experts believed children should grow up in their own racial environment. By the 1960s, however, the practice had become more accepted, though there was still apprehension, especially outside of major urban areas. Bob Fuhr, an insurance salesman, and Betty, a house-wife, had decided that it might be best if they didn't choose a mixed-race child. How could they honour their child's heritage without knowing anything about it? Would the child grow up to be lost in their white culture, adrift from his or her roots?

It was with this trepidation that Betty looked at the 18-day-old baby brought to her door by adoption officials. The child, said the official, had the Metis mark, a dark birthmark at the base of the spine that was thought to signify a child of mixed Native and white parentage. Betty understood what she was being asked to accept. "Trans-racially adopted children do not have the advantage of learning about their birth culture through everyday cues and bits of knowledge, assimilated almost unconsciously over years, as in single-race families," writes Jana Wolff, author of *Secret Thoughts of an Adoptive Mother* and the parent of a biracial child. "So the respon-sibility that parents have to their different-race children can seem overwhelming." It must have seemed that way for Betty, too. But whatever her fears, they were quickly overcome as she looked at the baby boy in the blankets. "The love was there," Betty later told *Sports Illustrated*. "It came to me."

A community of 18,000 with few non-white families, Spruce Grove was typical of small-town Canada in the 1960s. Settled by homesteaders in the 1870s, it was comfortable in its identity as a town on the railway line heading west out of Edmonton. The greater world that would intrude later that turbulent decade might as well have been a million miles away. In Spruce Grove, life revolved around the local hockey rink and the weekly broadcast of *Hockey Night in Canada* on Saturdays. The long, frozen months of a northern Alberta winter had to be endured until spring made its late appearance. Little wonder that the town's most notable athletic products—Grant, NHLers Stu Barnes, Nathan Dempsey and Ben Scrivens, plus Olympic gold medal skier Jennifer Heil—are all participants in winter sports.

While there were only a couple of black families in the area, Spruce Grove proved to be largely accepting of the active little boy with a passion for hockey. Betty and Bob later adopted Grant's sister Debbie, another mixed-race child. They accepted that they'd just have to cope with their fear of shortcomings. When Grant was four or five, his parents told him that he was adopted. Any concerns they had about him being unsettled were groundless.

Grant:
Probably being told that early—it didn't mean anything. The rest of the time growing up, you just saw them as your parents. It didn't really make much of a difference. At the time, you didn't know any better. While growing up all you knew is your mom and dad. That's all you worried about. They made sure you had whatever you needed. It was harder for

my sister, though, because she really wanted to know her parents. I think after Mom passed away she had mentioned it, and it didn't work out the way she wanted. Whereas I just assumed there's one set of parents and was treated that way. That's the way I was brought up. For me, I didn't know any better and didn't get treated any different. You don't realize, until you're a parent yourself, how much they gave up to give you everything. It reminds me of that saying, "Money isn't everything, but it sure keeps the kids in touch."

Bob and Betty worked hard to keep their active and energetic boy busy playing sports. Aside from part of a year spent in Saskatoon, home was 619 McLeod Avenue, a modest corner bungalow that, outside of the now-huge spruce tree on the front lawn, looks remarkably similar to the days when Grant was a child there. The garage that Bob built still stands. There was also an unfinished basement that served as a perfect indoor hockey surface.

Grant:

It wasn't a big house, but it was comfortable. Everyone sat in the living room and watched *Hockey Night in Canada* on TV. Everybody played. We could play hockey in the basement, because it wasn't finished. I think we drove Mom nuts, but we all kind of congregated there. And the other games kind of took place just out on the side street. There wasn't very much traffic except for the neighbours, so we played there and then ran across to play in the park. It was kind of a perfect spot. During the winter, you played hockey, summer baseball, sometimes field hockey. Drove the neighbourhood crazy while playing street hockey. Probably there were lots of neighbours that weren't very happy with us. But it was a perfect neighbourhood to grow up in. We had a whole bunch of different types. There were kids who were French. We had some Native kids. It was a wild mix of kids, but all die-hard athletes. Even the guys that weren't really athletically good still played.

For a boy more inclined to sports than studying, the park and the unfinished basement of the house on McLeod were the perfect laboratory. Betty was not athletic, but even she could see that her son was remarkably coordinated for his age. Teachers noticed, too. And so she accepted her son's 24/7 sports obsession.

Grant:
She liked it because it kept me out of trouble. So she would drive us wherever we needed to go. At that time I played baseball, hockey . . . hockey on a couple of different teams. Sometimes baseball on a couple of different teams. It was seven days a week doing something.

Against the backdrop of the long, cold northern Alberta winter, Grant became hockey obsessed. One night, at the age of seven, he told his family that he was going to play goalie in the NHL. "He said that more than once, too," remembered Betty Fuhr in a 1996 interview with *Sports Illustrated*. "Grant had a natural ability from a tender age. He was very well coordinated. He went to grade one, and the teachers were astounded at his coordination. Playing NHL hockey was a dream Grant had very early on. In concentrating on it so much, he never really liked school." The manifest hockey destiny was just fine with his father, a sports nut himself. Still, it fell to Bob, a former teacher, to make sure there was some balance in his son's life. That meant getting him off the rink and into his homework.

Grant:
He used to be a schoolteacher, so the school work for him was a big priority. I wasn't the best of students at that time. I banged heads with

him a few times over the years over that, because sports were my priority. A lot of the time you would have to have that homework done in order to play, so you found ways to do both things.

School was at Spruce Grove Composite High School. With the rink on the school grounds, it was easy to slip away during school. A lot of times they'd look to see which kids were missing and it was always the same kids. The vice-principal, Orest Haday, would walk over and knew exactly where to find us. It wasn't like they had to search hard. You got some kids that would go to the pool hall, and we were easy to find at the rink. We were always there. Well, then we'd get a little lecture about "Do you really think it's appropriate?" We'd be, "Probably not." He'd say, "Okay. Go back to the school," and we'd stay and play hockey. He'd just send me to the office and it would turn into a conversation about hockey. Our principal was another sports fan who was great. You might be in trouble but you were never in *real* trouble. A couple of the other teachers didn't quite see it that way. Mr. Haday took a lot of heat from them, but at the end of the day they also pushed you to be better. You just didn't realize it at that time.

The sports obsession that was natural to Grant, however, was less so for his sister.

Grant:

She probably got overlooked a little bit by the parents because sports dictated everything. In that sense, I'm probably not a very good older brother. She got dragged to a lot of baseball games, a lot of hockey games. I think she kind of got the bad end of the deal there and probably sacrificed a bunch. She got dragged to a lot of spots where I'd know she probably didn't want to be.

In addition to his family and friends in Spruce Grove, Grant had an extended family of cousins and grandparents living in nearby Stony Plain, Alberta. His grandparents (Gramps and Betty) lived together on a farm just outside of Stony Plain, right off of Highway 16. Grant still has many cousins out there: it's a big family, and they've all had kids. The *kids* have all had kids, too. Most of them still live around the Stony Plain area. Sunday visits to see the grandparents and cousins inevitably evolved into sports of some kind, with Grant and his cousins playing hockey, baseball or any other game that came to mind. Later, he would play those same sports against his cousins as a member of Spruce Grove teams taking on the boys from Stony Plain.

Grant:

Spruce and Stony was a pretty good rivalry. We had a lot of fun playing against Stony. It was kind of like Edmonton-Calgary, only the towns were a little bit closer. We always played minor sports against each other. We played minor baseball against each other. It was always kind of Spruce versus Stony. To go from that into Edmonton-Calgary wasn't that big a step.

Playing in tiny Spruce Grove had its advantages. As opposed to the big city of Edmonton, there was plenty of available ice in the small town and plenty of teams who could use a goalie. Grant was soon playing for multiple teams, often one or two age groups older. He'd occasionally fill in for his father's adult teams when the need arose for a goalie. The higher-calibre opposition pushed the young netminder to become faster in his reflexes and more calculating in his angles. Like so many NHL stars—such as future teammate Wayne Gretzky or Steve Yzerman—Grant's game was accelerated by the challenges of older competition.

While his fidgety self was in the classroom, Grant's mind was always on the sport he watched on TV every winter Saturday. With the Oilers not joining the NHL until 1979, he became a diehard fan of the Toronto Maple Leafs and their stellar goalies Johnny Bower and Terry Sawchuk. (He still calls Sawchuk, who starred in both Detroit and Toronto, the best goalie of all time. "He's always struck me as the guy who set the bar for everybody else with his style and his movement," Grant says.)

For an aspiring goalie, Sawchuk and Bower were the early role models—ironic since Grant's acrobatic style so little resembled their structured angles-first approach. Furthermore, Grant was left-handed, meaning he caught the puck with his right hand, the opposite of Bower and Sawchuk. Later, Grant would find more-similar models in Detroit's Roger Crozier and Chicago's Tony Esposito, both left-handed goalies who excelled at angles and agility in the 1960s and '70s. Being left-handed had its challenges for the young Fuhr: up until peewee, Grant had to make do with conventional gloves, playing the position cross-handed.

Grant:

I learned to play with flipped hands, so I actually caught with my left hand probably my first seven or eight years playing goal. I could still play that way if I had to. This one birthday, I finally got the set of gloves my natural way. Dad got them for me and it made things a thousand times easier, because it was just instinctive. I shot right-handed, so if you caught the puck, you could play the puck instead of letting it bounce. I felt pretty fortunate to get the gloves, and I seemed to get a lot better right away.

Neuroloigists talk about the flexible nature of a young brain that allows for dramatic leaps in cognitive and reactive abilities during the first two decades of life. This elasticity is why young people can change their hand preference or even their speaking accent after an accident—something virtually impossible to accomplish after the age of 20.

Grant's athletic style, mixing acrobatic movement with brazen courage, was soon the talk of the hockey community in Spruce Grove and nearby. Locals began discussing the pro prospects of Bob Fuhr's son. That notoriety also put him on the radar of Kenny Larue, a bird dog scout for the Victoria Cougars of the Western Hockey League, who operated Ken Den Crests in Edmonton. In the days before a bantam draft, most of the scouting was done by local men such as Larue, who passed on their reports to a particular junior team. Larue inquired whether the young lefty with the lightning hands and feet might be interested in playing for the Cougars. Grant didn't need to be asked twice.

Grant:
I drove out with my dad and my Uncle Roy, going to my first camp in Victoria. The first people we met in the office were Archie Henderson, Greg Tebott and Jim Clackson. As a 15-year-old kid, that was a little intimidating. At the same time, I didn't realize that it was going to be a career choice. It was just another level hockey to try out, to see if you liked it.

In the fall camp of 1978, Kenny Larue's impressive scouting report was validated: Grant was raw, but he impressed everyone with his competitive zeal and his blazing hand speed. Still, the Cougars had older goalies ahead of him on the depth chart, so that season Grant bounced back and forth between Victoria, his midget team in Spruce Grove and the Alberta Junior League. By his 17th birthday, however, he was in Victoria to stay. With a job assured in the Cougars' net, he dropped out of school to concentrate on becoming a pro goaltender. It was now the NHL or bust.

Grant:

I think the original plan was that we were going to take classes while I played junior—which lasted all of about half a year. The program we ran, coach Jack Shupe would practise at 11 o'clock every morning. It was run like a pro program. The big thing about Victoria was that it had a big-league atmosphere because, at that time, it was the only game in town. Plus we practised like an NHL team during the day. So you got to see what the pro game would be like. Some of the guys still managed to go through school, but mainly we just kind of treated it like, "Hockey's going to be it," and I stuck to that theory. At the time, you don't see it as a gamble. You look back at it now, it's a pretty big gamble. It was a big step, but my parents knew this is what I wanted and they were willing to give me a shot at following the dream.

The lovely harbour city of Victoria was a fortuitous place to land. Since entering the WHL in 1971, the Cougars had been a solid franchise (after a rocky debut). Despite a number of scoring stars and solid finishes, however, the team had never broken through in the post-season—even with future Blackhawk all-star Murray Bannerman in net. Grant's timing was perfect: he was the hero the Cougars were looking for. Grant was also fortunate to find himself alongside many stars who would go on to varying degrees of pro success. There was an authentic superstar in Barry Pederson, who became a Top-10 pick to Boston in 1980. In addition, the Cougars featured Greg Adams, highly touted first rounders Brad Palmer and Paul Cyr, enforcer Torrie Robertson and hard-nosed defenceman Bob McGill. Grant's draft season of 1980–81 was also the breakout WHL season of future NHL star Geoff Courtnall, who would be Grant's teammate in Edmonton's 1988 Stanley Cup run and from 1995 to 1999 in St. Louis. "We had a good team," Courtnall remembers. "We had a fast offensive team but defensively we weren't great. It was a run-and-gun team like Edmonton. [Grant] could stop two or three shots while the guys got back. I think in one of the games he had 50 shots. He just really made a lot of saves. The team won and lost based on how he played."

Many teenagers thrust into the high-stakes competition of major junior hockey far from home can experience extreme emotions of dislocation and stress. The transition for Native or black players can be even harder as they struggle to find a place both on the team and in a community usually unfamiliar with racial diversity. But with all the excitement of starting his junior career in a new city far from home, there was little time for Grant to become homesick.

Grant:

I wasn't ever homesick, but getting away from home was a little bit of an eye-opener. The family I billeted with was the McKaskills. Great household. Buddy McCarthy, Randy Zinn and I all lived in the same house. At the same time, the McKaskills had two kids with Down syndrome. It was an experience, and then to have us three fools running around made it even more interesting. All you did was live, breathe and die hockey.

For the first year, you're so preoccupied with playing that you don't understand that you're away from home that much until you get home around Christmas. My first road trip with the Cougars was 22 days by bus across the entire west of Canada. Play your way out to Winnipeg against the teams in Alberta and Saskatchewan, then play your way back from Winnipeg. We made the big swing though Alberta. You had to come back through Calgary, Lethbridge, Medicine Hat, so my parents would always make the full swing to see me play.

I think it was tough on my mom, though. She had a hard time with it, because right about that time, she and Dad got divorced. But I was away from it at the time, so I couldn't really tell. We talked on the phone all the time, so it didn't seem that bad to me. I didn't know any better except to play hockey every day. Leaving after Christmas is always hard, because now you got all this nice new stuff and it's got to stay at home till you get back at the end of the season in April or May. But the minute you're back with the guys on the team again, it's your built-in family.

Grant piled up the wins in his rookie season of 1979–80, going 30–12 while playing 43 of the Cougars' 72 regular-season games in his first year of major junior. He split time with holdover Kevin Eastman during the regular season, but the tandem produced the league's top goals against average (GAA) as Victoria allowed a whopping 67 fewer goals than anyone else.

A young Kelly Hrudey, playing for the Medicine Hat Tigers, had heard about the hotshot goalie who would become both an opponent and teammate in the NHL. "I had heard tons about him," Hrudey recalled. "He was a year younger than me, and I never knew what to expect about him. But in a league full of really athletic goalies, he had a better set of athletic skills at that level. And he used them. Not everyone did that. He relied on his catching hand all the time and he could recover with it. He was a pleasure to watch even then. You knew you had to be really good." Grant's almost perfect rookie season did not have a perfect ending, however. He suffered a dislocated shoulder on April 27 during the playoff game in which the Regina Pats defeated Victoria to win the WHL title. The shoulder woes were a precursor of ongoing issues he'd suffer during his NHL career, issues that led to pins being placed in his shoulders to hold them in place.

Grant's dynamic play garnered the Jim Piggott Memorial Trophy as the WHL Rookie of the Year for 1979–80. Better yet, for the first time, Victoria had made it all the way to the WHL final. The playoff breakthrough paved the way for the following season's success.

Grant's play left opponents and teammates in awe. "He had the perfect personality for a goalie," recalls Courtnall, who was called up to the Cougars midway through Grant's rookie year. "He was very calm and relaxed, not only in life but the way he played. He was a silent competitor. I was playing junior B and I hear that this goalie was up and coming and was one of the best coming up. In our playoff series, the reason why we got there was Grant."

For Grant, the following 1980–81 season would prove to be one of the best a goalie has ever had in the history of major junior hockey. Fuhr's Cougars owned the competition, setting a WHL record that still stands for wins (60) while outscoring opponents 462–217. Grant played 59 of the 72 games with numbers that sparkled by the high-scoring standards of major junior at the time: A GAA of 2.78, a save percentage of .903 and four shutouts—with a 48–9–1 record to go along with it. He led the entire CHL in every major goalie statistic possible and was given the Del Wilson Trophy as WHL Goalie of the Year.

So dominant was Grant that head coach Jack Shupe had this to say to reporters in December of 1980: "Maybe at times Grant shouldn't play so well. It would make the rest of the team work harder. They depend on him so much and take him so much for granted that it may be hurting us."

On occasion, Grant would challenge his whole team after practice. The players would have a competition where Grant would throw away his stick, each challenger would line up 10 pucks, and they'd play for a dollar a shot to beat him. At this time, Victoria had Brad Palmer, with an amazing shot, along with Barry Pederson, Courtnall and others. Even when Grant was playing without his stick, they still couldn't beat him. He'd just use his blocker and his catching hand and his feet. "He was incredible," says Courtnall. "He'd make money if they didn't score, so he did pretty well. Later, when we were in St. Louis, we'd do the same thing. But it was a little bit more expensive."

With the best overall record by far in the regular season, it was assumed that the Cougars would roll through the WHL playoffs toward the Presidents Cup and a berth in the Memorial Cup Tournament. But it almost didn't happen, as the Cougars found themselves down 3–1 in the WHL final to the Calgary Wranglers and future "Battle of Alberta" nemesis Mike Vernon. Behind Grant's clutch goaltending, however, the Cougars rallied. In a foreshadowing of the "money goalie" reputation that was to come in his NHL days, Fuhr bested Vernon in the remaining three games of the series. Following Grant's 30-save performance in the Game 6 win by Victoria, Shupe proclaimed, "Our goaltender came up big again. He's by far the best goaltender in junior hockey and he's showing it now."

Once at the Memorial Cup (a three-team tournament, held that year in Windsor, Ontario) things didn't go as well for the Cougars. After opening with a 7–4 win over OHL champs Kitchener, the Cougars dropped a 3–1 decision to the eventual winners of the tournament, the Dale Hawerchuk-led Cornwall Royals of the QMJHL. Then came a 4–2 defeat in the rematch with Kitchener. A semi-final return match with Cornwall went even worse as Victoria lost 8–4, finishing a disappointing third place.

The tough ending notwithstanding, Grant had turned the heads of scouts with his body of work in 1980–81. With the Memorial Cup over, the 18-year-old headed home to Spruce Grove to prepare himself for the rigours of the NHL entry draft process.

Grant:

Leading up to the draft, I didn't change anything. It was baseball season; hockey was over, so I started worrying about baseball. That was just my way of finding something to be competitive at. I caught, which was probably not the greatest thing. My dad found me a left-handed catcher's mitt, so I caught left-handed. If I wasn't catching, I'd play third base, where you're always kind of in the middle of everything. I could run pretty well then, too.

The interest in Grant, however, was decidedly from the hockey world. Grant had seen the scouts and agents hovering on the periphery, eager for a look at the hottest goalie prospect to grace the WHL in years. He was said to have the fastest hands—especially on the blocker side—and he handled the puck like a third defenceman. His save percentage was (for the times) an unworldly .903, while his peers were well below the .900 mark. It was the equivalent of being .940 in today's game. Scouts don't miss a thing like that.

Grant:

The scouts don't really talk to you afterward, but you know they're there. Not many people wear suits to junior games, so you know when the scouts are watching. If there are agents in town, there are scouts in town. But you weren't really worried—you just played. And we had a good team.

Grant eventually chose Frank Milne to represent him at the 1981 entry draft in Montreal. While Grant was widely projected as the top prospect in net (*The Hockey News* ranked him first at his position, 10th overall), no one was quite sure who'd jump first on the goaltending phenom. Goalies are notoriously fickle characters, and many organizations are gun-shy about using a top pick on a position that takes so long to mature. For every high first rounder who makes it, like John Davidson or Patrick Roy, there is a Jamie Storr or Brian Finley who disappears without a trace. Half of the goalies taken in the first round do not rise above backup status. Those who succeed often do so with a second or third team rather than the drafting club. The other problem (as blogger Kent Wilson points out) is that your goalie is either your most valuable player—on the ice at all times—or on the bench with a baseball hat on his head, doing nothing. No wonder that as the 1981 draft started, just 18 goalies had been taken in the top 10 in the previous dozen years.

Grant therefore faced some historical skepticism from the talent evaluators as the league convened in Montreal, much of it not of his own creation. Hawerchuk, whom he'd faced in the Memorial Cup, was the consensus No. 1 pick; after that, the draft order was a jumble, with Grant being mentioned alongside Bobby Carpenter, Ron Francis and Mark Hunter. But if you'd listened closely to Edmonton head scout Barry Fraser, you'd have gotten a hint about whom the Oilers had in mind with the No. 8 slot. "It's the worst draft year in the West in about 10 years," Fraser told Jim Matheson of the *Edmonton Journal*. However, Grant was going to be "the best goalie to come out of the draft since John Davidson." (At that point, Davidson was the star goalie for the New York Rangers.)

Fraser's boss, Oilers GM Glen Sather, was less sure. The four times Sather had seen Fuhr play he had been underwhelmed. "Are you sure you know what you're talking about?" he asked Fraser.

His head scout replied, "He's going to be in the Hall of Fame some day."

The draft, then held annually at the Queen Elizabeth Hotel in Montreal, was something less than the showbiz event it has now become. TV cameras were virtually non-existent, there were few if any fans in attendance, and the riches for being a top pick paled in comparison to the contracts handed out today. Furthermore, the techniques used to evaluate players were crude by today's standards of psychological profiling and aerobic testing at the combine. General managers depended on their trusted scouts (often pals from their playing days) and the NHL's Central Scouting assessments. Top overall selections often busted (Greg Joly, Doug Wickenheiser, Alexandre Daigle, Patrik Stefan), and excellent prospects could often be found in very late rounds or as free agents. Where might Grant fit in that lottery?

Grant:

I took only three days off to go down for the draft. They didn't choose the players [who attended] at that time the way they do now. You just went to the draft. Frank Milne just said, "You should probably come down." So I did. You went to the hotel ballroom, and all the guys were kind of sitting together. The guys I knew—Randy Moller, Marty Ruff, a bunch of the Alberta contingent—had all flown out on the same plane.

After Winnipeg took Hawerchuk, the Kings quickly followed with Doug Smith. Bobby Carpenter (Washington) and Ron Francis (Hartford) came next. When the Oilers' turn finally came at number eight, they had promising options: James Patrick, Tony Tanti, Al MacInnis, Steve Smith and Normand Leveille. Despite their enthusiasm for Grant, the Oilers brain trust understandably double-clutched at the draft table when Patrick, an impressive defensive prospect, fell to them. In 1981 the draft was a more rapid event, with picks going in without fanfare, and any delay was visible to onlookers. A hush fell over the ballroom: What would the Oilers do? But when the name went in, Sather opted for the acrobatic Fuhr from Spruce Grove by way of Victoria. While

Oilers fans had heard the Fuhr rumours, no one quite believed that the run-and-gun Oilers were going to stockpile another goalie after Moog's breakout performance in the 1981 playoffs. Patrick and MacInnis were a significant defencemen. Tanti promised goals by the bucket. There were other ways to go. The scuttlebutt had had Grant going to a number of cities.

Grant:

It was New York for the longest time: New York picked right after Edmonton. It was possibly Toronto, who picked right in front. Edmonton had never even been mentioned. It was a little bit of a surprise. Especially with Edmonton just finishing beating Montreal in the playoffs, and Andy having played so well. Edmonton wasn't even on the radar. Toronto or New York: I never really thought how my career might have been if I'd gone to those places. I did a fine job of getting in enough trouble here. I couldn't imagine. It might have been less trouble [in Toronto or New York], further from my comfort zone.

Al MacInnis was my roommate at the draft, because we both had signed with the same agent. I didn't know it back then, but I was going to be seeing and feeling his big slapshot for a long time. He played against me in Calgary and with me in St. Louis. I have the marks to prove it. There was also a group of us that had gone out from Alberta, like Randy Moller [drafted by Quebec] and Marty Ruff, who got drafted by St. Louis, I remember. We got to have a couple of drinks on the plane home afterwards with the Oilers announcer Rod Phillips, who had done the draft on radio. (If Roddy hadn't lied so much about me later I don't think I'd have made the Hall of Fame!) Then at training camp for the World Junior that summer my roommate was Kevin McClelland, who, even though we wouldn't have predicted it, was going to be my roommate for seven years with the Oilers.

Back home in Spruce Grove, Grant relaxed as always, playing baseball, golf and hanging out with his childhood buddies. It was a perfect summer to be the hottest goaltending prospect in the sport. Friends and family doted on the happy-go-lucky young man while the Edmonton media primed the pump for a rivalry with Moog. The next logical step for Grant seemed to be camp with Edmonton, then another year in Victoria with the Cougars. There was also the prospect of starting for Canada in the 1982 World Junior Championship, a tournament jointly hosted that year by the United States and Canada. With Scott Arniel, Marc Habscheid, Mike Moller and Gord Kluzak in their lineup, Team Canada was favoured for the gold medal. They did go on to win the tournament with a 6–0–1 record, but with Grant in Edmonton, Mike Moffat got the call in net instead, allowing just 14 goals. Grant would have to wait till 1984 to represent his country, then at the Canada Cup.

For many young players, missing a chance at gold in the WJC would be a disappointment, but for Grant, greater things lay ahead—even if he didn't know it as he headed to Oilers camp.

Grant agreed to his first contract in September 1981. It was a far cry from the million-dollar earnings he'd enjoy years later, but the three-year deal (plus an option year) at $45,000 per season and a $50,000 signing bonus must have seemed like a king's ransom to the humble youngster.

Grant:

I approached it as a junior player who was just happy to be in an NHL training camp. If they give me a contract, I'm as happy as can be. Slats always had his desk a little elevated above the chair you sat in. Talking to him, he's, "Oh. I've got a deal for you. It'll be great! This is what you get. If you don't like it, this is the extra you can get if you're good. There are no expectations. We don't know if you'll stay. We don't know where you fit. We don't know if we'll see you again. Enjoy your home town!" At that time, he's the general manager of a National Hockey League team. I'm, "Okay!" It was like winning the lottery. "At least I get a contract!"

That September, Grant discovered what it was like to be a professional in an NHL camp. There were details to take care of, big and small. Because his number of choice, 31, was occupied at the time by Eddie Mio, Grant needed a new number. After experimenting with 35 and 32, the Oilers gave Fuhr the more traditional goalie number of 1 (Grant would get 31 the following season, after Mio was traded to the Rangers). With that piece of business taken care of, it was then time to get to know his teammates. Grant had played with some of the guys growing up, and he had watched a lot of them on TV. But being on a team with Wayne Gretzky, Grant recalls, was about as good as it gets for a rookie.

Joining a team headed by the 20-year-old who would be the greatest offensive player in league history was like hitting a grand slam. The fire-wagon skill of the Oilers offence had been very much on display when Edmonton shocked the Canadiens in the opening-round sweep the spring before. "It was amazing to see them practise," says Mike Barnett, who would become the player agent for many of them, including Grant and Wayne Gretzky. "The speed and the way they threw the puck around was amazing. No one had seen anything like it before then."

Despite the out-of-nowhere performance from 21-year-old Andy Moog that post-season, Sather and his scouting personnel determined it was best to select a goalie who could hang with the lightning-quick style of the Oilers, which was to go up and down, attack, skate fast, but not really give a second glance to backchecking, defensive schemes or pinching defencemen. "If you compare our numbers with other teams it doesn't work," says Marty McSorley, "because we were scoring at such a high rate but also giving up goals at a high rate. We had a risk factor that is unheard of in today's NHL."

Upon entering the NHL, Edmonton was a scoring machine primed by Gretzky, but one that lacked big-game defencemen— relying instead on pluggers and retreads such as Lee Fogolin, Al Hamilton, Doug Hicks and Colin Campbell. Paul Coffey, drafted in 1980, would provide the catalyst on the blue line, moving the team from static to electric on the attack. The Oilers had shuffled goalies in and out like mad in their post-WHA phase, trying out Low, Dave Dryden, Jim Corsi, Eddie Mio and Gary Edwards. Until Moog's emergence, Mio had appeared to be the consensus "go-to guy." Now, here came the left-handed phenom from the Victoria Cougars, about to play in the NHL while conveniently living in his boyhood home.

Grant:

Slats made life easier. He said, "You're from here so you don't have to worry about getting a place." It's a lot easier transition where you're living at home. I had an easier time turning pro than playing junior, because junior I had to live out at a billet's place to go play. To turn pro I got to live at home. It wasn't so bad. I lived with Mom. I got home-cooked meals. Dad was in the city; Mom was in Spruce Grove still. I stayed out there for the first little while and then got a place in the city, but I still got to see everybody all the time. My uncles still had season tickets to the Oilers, so you'd see them every game. Everybody was always around, so it was normal. Except I was playing in the NHL.

My mom didn't say a word about me coming home late. "No, you're a big boy now. You've been away from home before so you can make your own decisions." That's how I teach my own kids. Life's learned by trial and error. If you're told you can do this and you can't do that, you're going to go see if you can do that or not. I found that out over the years. Somebody tells you it hurts if you grab a cactus, you're going to grab a cactus to make sure.

Though he was treated like an adult, being at home probably helped shield the young player from some of the pressures he might otherwise have faced alone. With so much going on around him, Grant stuck to the job of playing hockey, shutting out external noise as best as possible. That included the media reviews of how well he was performing in the Edmonton net.

Grant:

I played okay. I mean, it's hard to remember the games from training camp. Right up until the day they told me I was going to stick, I never really thought I would stick, because of all the guys there that had experience and how good Andy had been. But they must have seen something, because they kept me and let me start against Winnipeg in the fourth game of the season.

While the story of Grant's groundbreaking debut would likely be front-page news today, there is scarce evidence that his shattering of the racial barrier in net made headlines that night in Edmonton or anyplace else. Oilers fans were seemingly more concerned with how their team broke from the gate after the playoff success of the previous year. Besides, the advancement of racial minorities in hockey had seemingly never been high on anyone's list of priorities. Willie O'Ree broke the colour barrier as a forward when he played on January 18, 1958, for the Boston Bruins against the Montreal Canadiens. After two games that season in Boston he returned to the Bruins in 1961, scoring four goals with ten assists. "Racist remarks were much worse in the US cities than in Toronto and Montreal," O'Ree said afterwards. "Fans would yell, 'Go back to the South' and 'How come you're not picking cotton.' Things like that. It didn't bother me. I just wanted to be a hockey player, and if they couldn't accept that fact, that was their problem, not mine."

Racial progress was minimal in the sport. Despite the examples set by teams in other leagues, hockey organizations felt they could not employ players of colour. Toronto Maple Leafs owner Conn Smythe is reported to have said of another black player, Herb Carnegie, "I'll give any man $10,000 who can make Carnegie white." Legends such as Carnegie, who never got a shot in the NHL, were only hearsay to those who had never seen travelling negro hockey teams touring the country. Leafs Hall of Fame goalie Johnny Bower later alluded to the fact that, under owner Harold Ballard, drafting players of colour was not considered.

It wasn't until 1974 that Mike Marson became the second black player in the NHL when he skated with the Washington Capitals. He was followed in the 1970s by Tony McKegney, Bill Riley and Alton White. Those moments were significant for a black community that had been looking for role models. McKegney later talked about the challenge of not having a role model for his progress. "Sometimes I would wonder why I was trying to be a pro player when there were none to look up to. I'm proud of the fact that I was the first black to establish myself in the NHL. Now there are a few. I hope that helps youngsters who need someone to emulate."

But Grant's debut against the Jets in the fall of 1981 was the first time a black man had played in goal for an NHL club in a regular-season game. Grant was to prove different from those men who had blazed the trail for him; he would show that a black hockey player could not just make it, but could succeed at an elite level, given the opportunity. As usual, though, Grant was perhaps the least impressed person when it came to his history-making turn in net.

Grant:

I remember that first game mostly because I lost 4–2 to Winnipeg, and it was at home, which is never any fun. It was one of those things that wasn't supposed to happen. Your first game. You're not supposed to lose at all. I didn't really think about the other stuff.

Fuhr was bested in his debut by the Jets' newly acquired goalie, Ed Staniowski, fresh from languishing behind 1981 Hart Trophy runner-up Mike Liut in St. Louis. At the Oilers' end of the ice, Grant held his own, but he couldn't come up with what would become his signature save—foiling an opponent on the breakaway. Morris Lukowich beat him one-on-one at 16:12 of the second period for the winner. A final-minute empty netter by Lucien DeBlois meant Grant had allowed only three goals, a respectable total in those firewagon times, and one with which the Oilers usually won handily. Grant made 24 saves, but Staniowski was the difference maker, stopping 34 Oiler shots.

In what would become his usual reaction to a sloppy loss, Sather moaned and groaned about his team afterwards. "You spend thousands of dollars on scouting reports to get a feel for the other team, and then the guys don't believe what's written on the pages. . . . We definitely served up a turkey tonight," he quipped after the game—which came just after Canadian Thanksgiving.

Grant:

I actually don't remember the goals they scored that night. That's the great thing about being a goalie—you don't have to remember. You're like a relief pitcher in baseball or a cornerback in football: you can only think

about the next play. All I knew was I'd played in an NHL game. After the
game, I went out with my parents for something to eat at Coliseum Steak
and Pizza, which is kind of like a food staple in the city. The guys used to
go there all the time. It was a mixed feeling, sitting there after the game.
One, you're disappointed, but two, you're also happy to have played your
first game in the NHL. So it's kind of a six of one, half dozen of the other.
And for the next two or three days, you hear from everybody, because
you're playing an NHL game. Which, at least, I could always tell everybody
I played at least one game in the NHL.

Having made his debut and broken the goalie colour barrier,
Grant now had to get a win. Amazingly, the loss to the Jets was the
last time the rookie would taste defeat until well into the New
Year of 1982. Starting on October 21, when Grant backstopped
Edmonton to a 5–2 win over the Hartford Whalers, he etched his
name in the books with a 23-game unbeaten streak (15–0–8), a
record for a rookie netminder that remains to this day. It's also an
Oilers franchise record for a goalie of any experience. By the time
the winning streak was over, the NHL had taken notice of the kid
from Spruce Grove. Following an 8–3 win over the Pittsburgh
Penguins in the second game of the streak, Fuhr's prowess in
handling 35 saves prompted Pens head coach Eddie Johnston—a
former big league goalie himself—to remark to reporters, "If that's
an indication on the type of goaltender he's going to be, he's going
to be a great one."

After the next victory, a 5–3 decision over the Rangers during
which Grant stopped 37 pucks fired at him, Sather's appreciation
for his rookie's incredible focus was evident. "I thought Fuhr would
be nervous. But he's not affected by a lot. He's not affected at all."
To underscore his belief in Grant, Sather would demote Moog, the
hero of the previous spring's playoffs, to the minors to get some

work. Ron Low, at risk of being stolen off of waivers if exposed, remained to spell Grant in the Edmonton net.

Others in the goalie brethren were impressed by Fuhr as well. "I think Grant Fuhr reminds me of myself in the early part of my rookie year," praised Don Beaupre, a rookie sensation himself in 1980–81 and the second-youngest starting goalie to Grant at the time. "What I like about him, he's quick, he has really good concentration, he challenges the shooter and he's got a good [catching] mitt." In the midst of the undefeated streak, Fuhr was part of another milestone when he assisted on Wayne Gretzky's unprecedented 50th goal in 39 games. That historic moment came shortly after Grant returned from a dislocated right shoulder suffered on December 17, when Jamie Hislop of the Flames crashed into him. (Grant had suffered a dislocated or separated shoulder at least twice in his junior career, and the injury would start to shows its effects on his game as the season progressed toward the playoffs.) Grant had clearly overtaken Moog in terms of effectiveness.

The historic streak ended abruptly in Toronto on Grant's first visit to Maple Leaf Gardens, home of his boyhood heroes. Entering the building where Johnny Bower, Terry Sawchuk and Mike Palmateer had played was a thrill for the Oilers' aspiring goalie. But the result of the January game against a mediocre Toronto team was less thrilling.

Grant:
It was my first game at Maple Leaf Gardens, so it was pretty cool. Some games you do remember. That was one. After the first game with Winnipeg, I hadn't lost that season until that night: 7–1 on national TV in Maple Leaf Gardens. The Leafs weren't a very good team in those days, and a couple of those goals allowed were not very good. I had one go in from centre. I don't even remember who shot it: all I remember is

that I went to field it like a catcher and it bounced over my shoulder into the net. It was kind of the start of my evening. It was like, "Oh boy." We just didn't play very well.

So Slats made sure we paid penance the next day. We had a wonderful little skate, for an hour and 10 minutes, where pucks were not an option. It was kind of the "welcome to pro hockey" edition of the bag skate. You see it in junior all the time, but it was the first time I'd seen it in pro. Once you've paid penance, there's no reason to do that very often. You have your skate, the guys all go for a beer together, and it just brings the guys closer.

Later that month at the Capital Centre in Landover, Maryland, Grant received the prestigious starting nod in his first All-Star Game, after being named to the Campbell Conference team along with three of his teammates. The record unbeaten streak he'd put together would underscore a breakthrough season for the Oilers as a whole, with Grant finishing as runner-up for the Vezina Trophy (to Billy Smith) and Calder Trophy (to Hawerchuk). It was a rookie season on par with some of the greatest ever.

Grant:

It was a blur that year. You're just enjoying each moment of playing. You have no idea that it was close to a record or even near a record, because you're just you're happy that you're playing every day. As a kid, everything just blows by so fast. Especially an 18-year-old kid, your first year. You're not caring about winning or losing, you're just happy to be there playing in the best hockey league in the world.

Grant's final 3.31 GAA that season was among the league's best in just the third year after the NHL merger with the World Hockey Association, when jobs and opportunities were scarce. While the number sounds mediocre to modern ears, it was a stingy average in a league with a whopping average of 8.03 goals per game. The tsunami of scoring represented the NHL's highest scoring season between 1944 (when the Second World War diluted talent) and the present day. While his .899 save percentage and GAA would prove to be Grant's lowest for another 15 years, his final record of 28–5–14 was remarkable by the standards of any goalie, let alone a freshman netminder. Grant was often the impressionable type, for good or ill, and so he was quick to credit his roommate for his accelerated development.

Grant:

I had Ronny Low my first year, which really helped the transition of playing in the National Hockey League, because he'd been there for a while. So I got a little bit of an idea as to what to expect. He taught me angles, travel, all that stuff. Stuff that he'd overlooked on the way up, which, as an 18-year-old kid, you never think about. He made it comfortable and made it easy. He also had a great work ethic at practice. You'd see that and figure that's the way it's meant to be. That, you hope, wears off on you a little bit. And obviously, later, it was the same with Andy, who, because we pushed each other, made each of us better. You go from Ron to Andy to Bill Ranford—same thing. All the way along, you get pushed to be better, which is the best way of coaching.

Fuhr's phlegmatic approach was famously observed by author Peter Gzowski in his book *The Game of Our Lives*. "He would answer questions as if he had never learned the art of the 'interview'—the ritual by which hockey players would phrase wordy and predictable answers to wordy and predictable questions. Fuhr answered what was asked of him, no less but certainly no more. Asked if he found NHL play much tougher than junior A, he would not say, as the ceremony demanded, 'Well, they're faster here and they shoot harder and I'm playing against guys I used to read about and dreamed of playing against, but I just try to do my job one game at a time, and if I hang in there I think. . . . Instead, he answered 'no.'"

Through his miracle rookie season, Grant's unflappable nature became a standard tale for reporters. A *Sports Illustrated* article on the Oilers of 1981–82 illustrated a typical conversation with the 19-year-old:

> "Grant, do you get excited about anything?"
> "Not really."
> "Why not?"
> "There's not a whole lot to get excited about."

"I've never seen anyone like him," added Glen Sather in the same article. "He never gets rattled or shakes his head or panics." Oiler winger Dave Lumley was astonished, too. "A puck may have just whizzed by his head, and all Grant will say is, 'Hmm, that was an interesting shot.'" Grant went out and proved in 1981–82 that all the ink the press had been using to extoll his coolness under pressure was not being wasted on clichés. It was dead on. His first game was a milestone on several levels. It was notable because of his age, his colour, and because it was the last time the pro hockey world would look at Grant Fuhr as just another goalie prospect.

GAME 2

They say a week is a long time in politics. The same applies for NHL goaltending. In the eyes of the fans, a couple of poor games in a short span can transform a netminder from a hero to a punchline. A bad few months of play, especially before the home fans, can be fatal. The 1982–83 sophomore season Grant experienced in Edmonton is all the proof one needs of the transient nature of fame for an NHL goalie. The flashy reflexes and uncanny anticipation that characterized his rookie year were suddenly a thing of the past. The raucous cheers heard so often from Oilers fans the year before had morphed into catcalls. As reporters surrounded the second-year Oilers netminder in the dressing room following a dispiriting 4–3 loss to lowly Detroit, scribes who'd once extolled the unflappable Grant Fuhr had to double-check their notepads. This angry 20-year-old was anything but the what-me-worry Fuhr of his breakthrough rookie campaign.

The fickle nature of the fans at Northlands that night had not played well with No. 31. "I'd like to get the fans out of my system," Grant growled following the loss. "I could care less what they want to do . . . they're all jerks. I've given up on them. . . . The fans here are all over my case. . . . I've not had good luck in this building. For me it's a lot easier to play on the road than here."

Grant was correct when he moaned to the media about being haunted in his home rink. While Grant played acceptably on the road in 1982–83, games at Northlands seemed to have brought out the worst in him.

Grant:

I was not very good. And at 19 years old, you're not sure how to deal with not-very-good. So, of course, we stuck our foot in our mouth about the fans to get off to a flying start. We'd played the Jets a few nights before. That night I tripped over the back of the net going to stop a puck, and it hit my stick. It bounced out in front of the net. It was one of those highlight goals. Then one banked in off the glass from centre as I was going behind the net. I didn't move to stop it, it bounced off the Plexiglas. So I had two goals go in while I'm sitting behind the net. That was not very good. We played a few nights later at home, and lost 4–3. To Detroit—not a very good team. Then after the game I called the fans jerks. Yes, "jerks" would be the exact term I used. Obviously I vented a little. It might have been the only time that I didn't think before I spoke that year.

The boys got a good chuckle out of me on that one. I learned from it, though. When I came back I got even quieter. Because I figured if you're not sure what you're going to say, don't say anything. Or answer in one or two words. And I got pretty guarded for a lot of years after that. I wasn't going to get us in trouble again.

With the Edmonton media baying for a solution to the Oilers' suddenly poor goaltending, GM Glen Sather summoned Grant to his office for a chat. In the course of the one-sided discussion, Sather fulfilled Grant's desire to play away from Edmonton for awhile, sending him on a prolonged road trip. This wasn't a road trip with the Oilers, however: following a 4–3 loss to the Vancouver Canucks on January 22, the rookie flash was assigned a 10-game stint with the Oilers' AHL affiliate, the Moncton Alpines. There, *all* the games would be road games.

Grant:

Slats called me in, and we had a little conversation about things you should and shouldn't say. It was like you did something wrong, and then you were scolded for it. (At least I only called the fans jerks—Messier missed a plane one time.) I don't think he was very happy. I got myself a really nice middle seat to the farm team in Cape Breton so I could get away from the pressures of Edmonton, find my game, and get my head back to where it's supposed to be. Just go down to Sydney, jump on the bus, ride around a little bit, get to see some of the nice places that the American League has to offer—then realize that that's not where you want to be.

Messier's dad was coaching there. And I had played for him before with the Spruce Grove Mets. Messier's brother Paul was playing there, too. So it was a comfortable place to be from that standpoint. I was there for about two weeks, playing games and keeping quiet, and then came back. I only played another four or five games in Edmonton that season. I watched Andy Moog play a lot. It was more frustrating for me, because I'd got comfortable with everything going on the year before, and I expected it was going to keep going well. And, more than anything, I had a hard time figuring out why it *wasn't* going well.

Perhaps his loss of confidence in Edmonton dated back to the 22 pucks that had gotten by him in three dreadful playoff losses against the Los Angeles Kings the spring before in the 1982 play-offs. The embarrassing performance against the Red Wings that January night in 1983 was a harsh reminder of how Grant and the highly favoured Oilers had folded against a mediocre foe during the post-season. Memories of that collapse no doubt inspired boos from the normally supportive Oilers crowd.

Following the Oilers' impressive upset of Montreal in the spring of 1981, many had thought the high-scoring team would, at the very least, be in the Campbell Conference finals, if not taking a turn as the Islanders' dance partner in the Stanley Cup finals of 1982. It was a classic case of putting the fire wagon ahead of the horses. Like all disasters, it started simply enough: with a "warm-up" against the Los Angeles Kings, the lowest-ranked of all 16 post-season clubs. The Kings had finished the regular season with a whopping 48 fewer points than the Oilers (63 to Edmonton's 111) in the Western Conference standings. Adding to the Oilers' confidence was the fact that Edmonton had also dominated the Kings in the regular season, winning by baseball scores of 7–4, 11–4, 5–1, 10–3, 6–2 and 7–2 in six of the eight meetings. A walk in the park for Edmonton, said the critics, ignoring a few small details. The Kings were loosey-goosey, as most underdogs tend to be, playing the Oilers as if they had nothing on the line. After a season of success, Grant and his defence suddenly looked (and felt) like the ones who had everything to lose.

And lose they did. The tone was set with a wild 10–8 Kings victory in Game 1 (still the NHL record for most combined goals in a playoff contest). The game revealed an Oilers club that seemingly had forgotten about defence and was bent on wearing out the nets behind the two goalies. Edmonton barely survived Game 2, with a 3–2 overtime victory over a Kings team whose cockeyed confidence was growing by the minute.

Then came the game that would be forever known as "The Miracle on Manchester" (so named for the Los Angeles street on which the Great Western Forum stood). The Oilers got out to an easy 5–0 lead, seemingly playing with a hand tied behind their back. But then the tone of the game changed. The Oilers' 34-year-old veteran centre, Garry Unger, took a five-minute high-sticking major that spurred an L.A. comeback. Before a delirious home crowd, L.A. stormed back in the third period to tie the score in regulation time. With Grant and the Oilers stunned by such a rapid change of fortune in the final 10 minutes of play, the Kings got a goal from unsung Daryl Evans to win 6–5 in OT. It was— and remains—the biggest blown lead in the post-season history of the team.

Grant:

It was a "last shot wins" game. There weren't very many saves made. It was one of those games where the harder you chased it the farther away it got from you. The lovely Miracle on Manchester. That was the [Kings] franchise's only highlight till then: even when I got traded there in 1995, they still played it before every game. It's not the highlight that you want to see when you're coming out of the locker room.

The Oilers managed to avoid elimination with a 3–2 win in Game 4, setting up a winner-take-all scenario back home for Game 5 (the opening round was a best of five at the time). The team was forced to fly back to Edmonton on the same charter flight as the Kings for the deciding game. In a move typical of the Oilers' hubris, the team brass (feeling that they would have the series taken care of in three or four games) had neglected to book their own charter and had to go cap in hand to the Kings to hitch a ride back to Alberta. Charlie Simmer, a part of the Kings' Triple Crown line with Marcel Dionne and Dave Taylor, chuckled as the Oilers filed onto the plane. "We heard that Glen Sather wanted the Oilers to get the front seats on the plane," he recalled years later.

"But our owner, Mr. [Jerry] Buss, told them to get to the back of the plane. We enjoyed that."

Fittingly, the Kings took the Oilers for another bumpy ride on the Northlands ice in Game 5, racing out to a 7–2 lead over their stunned opponents. The Kings then coasted home, winning the Smythe Division semi-final with a score of 7–4. Edmonton had only themselves to blame for wasting the home-ice advantage in the deciding game. To Sather's consternation behind the bench, his club took foolish penalties early that resulted in two power play goals for the Kings. While Sather's team held superstar Marcel Dionne at bay, unheralded players like Daryl Evans, Bernie Nicholls, Doug Smith and Steve Bozek scored some of the biggest goals in the series.

The Kings hadn't won in Edmonton all year heading into the series, and yet they did so twice in three playoff meetings at Northlands. The 48-point disparity between that underdog series winner and the favourite they toppled is the widest in NHL history. Grant, a few months shy of 20, didn't look particularly sharp in the series: his GAA was a bloated 5.05. The focus was not on Grant's shortcomings alone, however; as a team, Edmonton had looked lost and undisciplined. The freewheeling Oilers treated defence like an option against the Kings, whose upset was the L.A. franchise's only series victory between 1977 and 1989.

Grant:

All I remember is, it was my first playoff and we lose 10–8 the first game, win 3–2, win 3–2, then lose 6–5 in overtime, then lose 7–4. I thought, I'm not going to be here very long if that's the way the playoffs are going to go. We should have beat L.A. Wow, I didn't play very well in that playoff series. That Game 1 was a nice eye-opener for me about playoff hockey in the

NHL. But it got worse. Much worse. The Miracle on Manchester. Then we lost at home in Game 5 to a team we'd owned in the regular season. Not a great way to go into the summer.

––––––––––

The run-and-gun style of the 1981–82 Edmonton Oilers and super-star Wayne Gretzky had received almost all of the attention from the press and hockey media. That was how Sather wanted his team to be known. In several memorable WHA series with the Winnipeg Jets, he had seen the opponents' influx of European players (such as Anders Hedberg and Ulf Nilsson) at work. Their style made an impression, and influenced Sather to turn the Oilers into a similarly freewheeling club when he graduated from journeyman player to Edmonton's head coach in 1976. (Sather's admiration for how the Jets changed hockey was demonstrated over the years as he brought in former Jets such as Willy Lindstrom and Kent Nilsson, and even former Jet defender Ted Green as one of his assistants.) Sather believed that, unlike previous NHL dynasties, the Oilers could excel with an uptempo game that didn't rely on conservative check-ing strategies. But the major stroke of luck came, of course, when a 17-year-old stick figure named Wayne Gretzky fell into the Oilers' lap. Gretzky's club, the WHA's Indianapolis Racers, were undergo-ing hard times in the fall of 1978, and before the concerned parties could enter into any dispersal draft, Oilers owner Peter Pocklington purchased the contracts of Eddie Mio, Peter Driscoll and Gretzky for a now-laughable sum, reported to be anywhere from $700,000 to $850,000. Sather then managed to keep Gretzky out of the NHL draft and expansion redistribution of players.

The magnificent Gretzky had made the Oilers the darlings of the media crowd. What went largely unnoticed, however, was how Grant had handled the burden of being left alone at the other end, bailing out the offensive juggernaut in 48 of the Oilers' 82 games in his first year. But in year two, when cracks began showing in Grant's confidence, he and the team began searching for an explanation. His rookie campaign of 1981–82 had been such a revelation; most felt he would learn from the disastrous playoff experience against the Kings and move ahead from there. But now, the 1982–83 season was looking like more of the same.

Grant:

When you're that age, you can't possibly see how things wouldn't keep going on forever the way they'd gone the year before. It was still the same game and the same puck. But by the time I went down to Cape Breton it felt like everything was different.

Grant was discovering what so many before him had learned about the vagaries of being an NHL goalie. There were only two dozen starting jobs in the world at the time; if you lost yours, it was often impossible to get it back. When asked why he chose goaltending as a profession, Grant's hero from Toronto, Johnny Bower, explained the mindset: "I just made up my mind I was going to lose teeth and have my face cut to pieces. It was easy." Another goalie from Grant's youth, Roger Crozier, had won a Conn Smythe Trophy for his clutch playoff performance in 1966, but he, too, constantly battled the uncertainty of the position. "I like everything about hockey," Crozier told writer Jim Hunt. "The travelling, the friends I've met, the interviews. I like everything but the games." After losing three games in 1969, Crozier quit to work as a carpenter back home, finally returning to the game after being traded to Buffalo. Perhaps the most perceptive goalie ever, Ken Dryden, summed up the goalie's dilemma in his classic book *The Game* when quoting his former peer in the Montreal farm system Tony Esposito. "The pressure is unreal. Most of the goalkeepers, they feel the pressure. The only ones that don't worry are the ones too dumb to understand what's happening to them."

Former *Vancouver Sun* columnist Jim Taylor had a more droll explanation for the pressure: "Any discussion on hockey goaltenders must begin with the assumption that they are about three sandwiches shy of a picnic. I can prove this. From the moment Primitive Man first lurched erect, he and those who came after him survived on the principle that when something hard and potentially painful comes at you at great velocity, you get the hell out of its path. Goalkeepers throw themselves into its path. I rest my case."

Those pressures of goaltending affect different men in different ways. While Grant was largely placid during his long career, his fellow Albertan and Hall of Famer Glenn Hall used to throw up before games. Esposito bathed himself in Rub A535 liniment. "Suitcase" Gary Smith shed his bulky padding and showered between periods. Canadiens legend Jacques Plante knit his own toques and sweaters. Many of the men who faced vulcanized rubber whistling past their ears were raging drunks, others brooding loners. Gilles Gratton, a goalie in the '70s, might have been the strangest ever: he thought he was playing goal to atone for having stoned people in a previous life.

What was a teenager like Grant, fresh from junior hockey, supposed to do in the face of such stories? There were no goalie coaches per se in the NHL in 1982. Grant's first goalie coach wouldn't come till his stay in Buffalo in the 1990s, when Mitch Korn was his mentor. Most NHL head coaches let goalies work it out for themselves away from the rink. So while his team was rebounding from the devastating end to the previous year's playoffs, Grant was trying to reclaim his mojo all on his own. Then came his public blast at the Edmonton fans midway through the 1982–83 season. By the time of his demotion to Cape Breton, Grant was barely at a

.500 winning percentage. It was hard to reconcile the remarkable rookie of 1981–82 (who'd finished runner-up to Dale Hawerchuk for the Calder Trophy) with the inconsistent, irritable goalie in his sophomore campaign.

Grant's sophomore dilemma is not uncommon for athletes, says the University of San Francisco's Dr. Jim Taylor (no relation to the columnist). "You start to get nervous before a competition because you believe you will perform poorly," he writes. "All of that anxiety hurts your confidence even more, because you feel physically uncomfortable and there's no way you can perform well when you're so uptight. The negative self-talk and anxiety causes negative emotions. You feel depressed, frustrated, angry, and helpless, all of which hurt your confidence more and cause you to perform even worse. . . . As bad as you feel, you just want to get out of there. If you're thinking negatively, caught in a vicious cycle, feeling nervous, depressed, and frustrated, and can't focus, you're not going to have much fun and you're not going to perform well."

The rough transition in 1982–83 was brought on, in part, by Grant's relaxed attitude toward preparing for a new season. He had (against Sather's wishes) refused to rehab his balky shoulder properly after off-season surgery, and he was chastised for poor conditioning when he showed up at Oilers training camp. Even Grant conceded that he came into his second NHL season 20 pounds overweight from an off-season of inactivity thanks to the ailing shoulder, and also because he "loved to eat." Now living on his own in Edmonton, there was none of Mom's home cooking; it was junk food and late-night snacks.

Grant:

I got my shoulder glued back together that summer. I couldn't rehab for about the first eight or ten weeks, and then didn't really rehab the way it probably should have after that. And it added some pounds that probably didn't need to be there. Then, as the season began, I had the opposite problem. I'd lost a bunch of the summer weight when the year started. I was lighter even than what I had carried my first year. I was almost too light. Now you get tired faster and have no strength. So I'd gone from one extreme to another extreme, and couldn't find the happy medium.

I got frustrated with that. I was quick, but with no stamina. And as you were thinking about all this, the puck was getting by you. The minute you think about what you're doing as a goalie, you're late. Doesn't matter how fast you are. Playing goalie, you can't think the game—you have to *play* the game. You can think afterwards and before, but you can't when you're playing. It just has to happen. So that was my first experience of thinking my way through the game. Not so good. I got off to a sluggish start. The team started slowly too. And things steamrolled from there.

For the first, but not the last time in Grant's career, conditioning was a battle with authority. This time it was over baseball, a sport Grant played well enough as a catcher to get professional offers. It was his summer fallback sport (until golf came along).

Grant:

The only thing that really changed, fitness-wise, is that I liked to play baseball in the summer, and that was overruled by Slats about two weeks into my training camp: I got summoned to the office and told that there would be no more baseball. I had turned my ankle and that didn't go over very well. We bent that rule the next year and played fast pitch. That got overruled pretty quickly too. But that was my way of staying in shape in the summer. Baseball kept your eyes sharp and gave you the opportunity to play. You're competitive at something. You're never really getting out of the competitive edge.

At the start of the 1982–83 season, the malaise affecting Grant seemed to have somehow crept straight through the locker room. Expecting to own the NHL as they'd done the previous year, the Oilers nevertheless got off to a disappointing 4–6–3 start through October, allowing a surprising 65 goals in those 13 games. Fuhr and Andy Moog were suddenly struggling to cover up for poor defence. After losing the starting job in the playoffs to Fuhr in 1982, Moog was now the more effective of the two Edmonton netminders. Finishing with a 33–8–7 record, a 3.54 GAA and a .891 save percentage, Moog got the bulk of the starts that season. Grant, meanwhile, suffered through slumps that produced a mediocre 13–12–5 record with an ugly 4.29 GAA and a .868 save percentage (not wretched numbers on a shoot-'em-up team like the Oilers, but still not up to anyone's expectations or standards).

In the midst of the disappointment, however, the Fuhr/Moog tandem actually cemented a successful routine that would exist in the Edmonton net until Moog was dealt to Boston in 1987.

Grant:

Andy was a couple years older than me, and I'd played against him in junior. He was in Billings [Montana, with the Bighorns], and he was very good. We were going to split the season 50-50 [in 1982–83], and we did most years. I just happened to get lucky, to be able to play in the playoffs [in 1982]. That first year, I played and didn't have a very good playoffs. Andy started the playoffs in my second year, and I thought he had a really good playoff, and I got lucky to play in the third year. Things turned out pretty well, so, it kind of ran from there. It could've just as easily been Andy.

Andy was more a butterfly guy. I more moved around a little bit, and relied on reflexes and tried to just figure it out as I was swimming around. You watch your defencemen, you see how they handle things, you try and figure out what they're doing that makes you better. In the first few years, my style was all reflexes. A lot of it may have come from playing baseball, and catching, where everything's based off you being in a crouching position, and having to be explosive from there. That kind of rolled in to goaltending. As you learn, you can control it a little bit more and you move a little bit better. The biggest thing I figured out after that second year was, as you start to struggle, your instinct is to get closer to the net. You think you can rely on what's your best instinct, reflexes. But if you're standing on your goal line at five foot nine, 180 pounds, you're not taking up very much net. Guys in the National Hockey League are pretty good; if you give them that much net it doesn't matter how fast you are. So even though the farther you got from the net the worse you felt, the result was actually better.

While Grant's sophomore year didn't come anywhere near his later standards, the Oilers did recover from their slow start. Edmonton took advantage of the Smythe Division's weakness and caught fire, finishing 47–21–12 for 106 points and third place in the entire NHL, just behind the Flyers and Bruins. Once more, fans and the media were talking about just how far Glen Sather could take his team in the playoffs. But that 1982–83 regular season ended with Moog logging almost all the minutes in net, and despite the Oilers' turnaround, Grant was left to contemplate the riddle of where his game had gone.

Grant:
I couldn't quite put those two pieces together that year. You feel lonely, but you get really frustrated. Up until then, I never had a struggle before. And then it just kind of happened. And for the life of me I couldn't figure out how to fix it.

But even though I struggled, I still got to play. I had my feet underneath me by the time I came back from the minors. It wasn't like I was going to sit the rest of the year. I got the opportunity to be in the net, probably not as much as I would like, but about as much as I deserved. Slats kept letting me play. I was able to get my confidence back.

Other coaches might have nailed Grant to the bench, if only to preserve their jobs. But Sather had the advantage of being both coach and general manager. It allowed him to see the short term and the long term for his club. That meant investing in Grant even when he might cost his team a game. Coming to the Oilers was a fortunate outcome for Grant, who might have drifted into obscurity if left to his own devices in another organization. This crisis of confidence was just the first of many situations Sather and Grant would navigate in his Edmonton career.

Grant:

Slats kind of moulded us and gave us enough rope to hang ourselves. Then, at the last second, he reeled us back in. He was more like a father to us than anything. He let you get away with stuff that you probably shouldn't have. But then he pulled you back. It was never a good sign when you got summoned to his "castle" [Sather's office], because you had to go up the stairs in the back of the Coliseum to get up there. You always knew you were in trouble when you headed to practice by going up the back stairs first. And everybody can see you going up those back stairs. You worked out much harder in practice if he saw you in his office before, not after, you skated. Which at the time we never realized. Pretty good thinking by Slats, because you'd be that much better at practice.

Grant took a seat on the bench for the Oilers' run to the Cup finals in 1983, coming into a game only once during the 16 games (he was subbed into a 10–3 thrashing of the Calgary Flames in Game 4 of the 1983 Smythe Division final). He watched from the bench as Edmonton turned heads the way fans and critics had expected them to do in 1982, demolishing their first three opponents in the Campbell Conference en route to the Cup final. The Oilers posted an 11–1 record while outscoring Winnipeg, Calgary and Chicago by a laughable 74–33 margin—all with Moog performing solid duty instead of Grant. But even Moog at his best couldn't save Edmonton from the harsh lesson of the finals, where they met the battle-scarred New York Islanders, the latest incarnation of a dynasty gunning for a fourth consecutive championship.

While many believed the meeting with the upstart Oilers was going to spell the end of an Islanders championship run that had started in 1980, Al Arbour's team still had some fight left. The stick-wielding head games of Islanders star goalie Billy Smith distracted the young Oilers. In particular, Gretzky, unsettled by a slashing incident with Smith, ended the series goal-less. Edmonton's fire wagon offence was neutralized to just six goals in four games by the Isles' suffocating defence, relentless forechecking and Smith's Conn Smythe–winning goaltending. As Grant watched helplessly, the Isles engineered a surprising sweep, dealing out some valuable lessons in the process. Smith—relishing the victory and rubbing salt in the Oilers' wounds—then quipped to *Hockey Night in Canada* (within earshot of league president John Ziegler) that when he slashed Gretzky in Game 1, No. 99 had gone down as if shot.

While his off-ice troubles would be a distraction during the decade, Grant's play would rarely waver after 1982–83. He gained confidence as he progressed during the following season, stepping once again toward respectability following that sophomore slump. And Grant's road to reclaiming his status as a future goaltending great would coincide with a shift in the overall team mentality: everyone was looking to rebound from the jarring Cup final defeat at the hands of the Islanders. With eyes fixed on the No. 1 goalie position, Grant was swept up in the excitement of the Oilers' new expectations—going for the trophy that owner Peter Pocklington had so boldly predicted would be in their grasp within five years of entering the NHL. There was just one place to start that process: a rematch with Billy Smith and the Islanders.

GAME 3

Most champions can point to a crucial moment when potential turned to production, when riddles became titles. The Montreal Canadiens of the 1970s, arguably the greatest NHL teams of all time, point to a pre-season game against the defending Stanley Cup champion Philadelphia Flyers in 1975 when the Habs matched the Broad Street Bullies punch for punch, deflating forever the myth of the Flyers as all-conquering bullies. The Habs then reeled off four straight Cups, while the Flyers simply reeled away. Later, the New York Islanders slew the dragons of repeated playoff failures in the late 1970s when GM Bill Torrey dealt popular veteran Billy Harris (a former No. 1 overall pick) and Dave Lewis to acquire centre Butch Goring. With a legitimate No. 2 centre, the Isles then won 19 consecutive playoff series (unmatched in the history of professional sports) and four straight Cups themselves.

For Grant and the heralded young Oilers, their own playoff disappointment against those Islanders stung to the core in 1983. To make the humiliation worse, the defeated Oilers had been forced to file past the celebrating Islanders dressing room after the clinching Game 4. As they say in boxing, to become a champion you must

49

beat a champion—and heading into the 1983–84 playoffs, the Isles were the heavyweight champs of the post–WHA merger NHL. The Long Island crew stood between the Oilers and their destiny.

The Isles had been working their mastery over Edmonton for a while. Not only had they beaten the Oilers in a brief 1981 quarter-final and then the 1983 final sweep, but from December of '81 through the 1984 regular season, the Islanders had also recorded an 11-game unbeaten streak against Edmonton. Even though the Oilers had topped the NHL's overall standings with 119 points (14 more than the Bruins and Islanders, in second and third place respectively), they were just paper champions until they proved they could subdue Al Arbour's team.

After a smooth passage though the first three rounds of the 1984 post-season, the Oilers' chance for redemption came in the final. It was a match the entire league anticipated. Whatever the regular-season statistics, Gretzky, Mark Messier and Fuhr would still be playoff underdogs against Bryan Trottier, Mike Bossy, Denis Potvin and Billy Smith. As Grant and his teammates skated out to meet the Isles the night of Game 1, the pressure of being the NHL's top team in the regular season also weighed heavily: only 9 regular season winners since 1983–84 have actually won the big prize. As he waited through the national anthems, Grant saw at the other end of the ice a champion team showing its age—but with plenty of veteran savvy left as well. The legendary Bill Torrey had augmented his veteran core of Trottier, Bossy and Potvin with young blood in the form of Pat LaFontaine, Pat Flatley and Gord Dineen. After narrowly escaping defeat in the opening round of the playoffs at the hands of the New York Rangers (who had upset them back in 1979), the Isles had steamrolled to a return date with the Oilers.

For Grant, there was a much riding on the showdown. With a

clutch performance here in Game 1, Grant had the chance to supplant Andy Moog as Glen Sather's go-to goalie in crucial post-season games. That would represent a singular turnaround from the previous spring, and few who'd seen the struggling Fuhr of 1982–83 would have guessed that the 21-year-old could come back from his sophomore blues to earn Sather's trust once again. But a string of 17 starts in 21 games (going 14–6–2) from October to December of 1983 signalled the return of the workhorse from his slump. He and Moog fairly evenly split the workload during the regular season in 1983–84: Fuhr played in 45 games while Moog drew into 38, demonstrating the confidence the Oilers brass had with either option.

Their performances were nearly identical playing within the run-and-gun Oilers hockey system. Moog owned the superior GAA (3.77 to Grant's 3.91) while Grant had a slightly higher save percentage (.882 to Moog's .881). Both had put up sparkling win/loss records (30–10–4 for Grant, 28–7–1 for Moog) and finished Top 10 in the Vezina Trophy voting. During the regular season, Grant had also toppled the league record for assists by a goalie, posting 14 (six more than the previous mark set in 1980–81 by Mike Palmateer of Toronto). The Edmonton goalie tandem surrendered 314 goals—but that was still good enough for the 10th-fewest allowed in the scoring-mad 21-team league where Gretzky and friends pillaged defencemen and goalies with their wizardry.

Marty McSorley wasn't to become an Oiler till 1985, and he well remembers his time in Pittsburgh, and the intimidation factor of facing Edmonton in those days. "They were so fast. Teams would ice the puck thinking they could get a rest and make a change. But Fuhrsie would race to the corner and one-touch the puck up again and be on them right away." Playing with Grant was an entirely different story. "He was so consistent, so accountable, it was fun to play him in practice, because he would challenge you. Nowadays you look around and you can say that the best athlete is in net. Back then it wasn't that way. But with Fuhrsie you had a really good athlete. He'd poke-check a guy lying on his belly and then be standing up and take the rebound in his chest. He was really athletic in a time when not all the goalies were."

With their two goalies reliably minding the cage, Edmonton's corsairs up front smashed their own scoring record, tallying 446 goals—a record surely never to be topped in the current defensive-minded NHL. All that was needed to cement their greatness was a Stanley Cup.

Grant:

We were a loaded team without realizing it, because everybody played and had fun every day. I mean, Gretzky was special—everyone saw that each night. And we got to see it in practice every morning: sometimes he was just as impressive in practice because he didn't like to lose. But the rest of us were still a bunch of wide-eyed guys, like Mess. I used to practise with Mark's team back as a kid, so I knew he was good. They brought in Glenn Anderson from the Olympic team: I played against him in the playoffs when I was in Victoria and he played for Seattle, so we knew Glenn was good. Paul Coffey had rave reviews in junior—obviously a first-round pick—so he can play. Jari Kurri was as good a two-way player as there was. He didn't know it at that time, but he knew to shoot the puck and score. Lee Fogolin was a great leader on defence: he and Kevin Lowe kept it together back there. We had a bit of all the things you need to win.

Grant's comeback was one of those things the Oilers needed in the successes of the 1983–84 season. His perseverance in recovering from the disastrous previous season had paid off quickly when he was selected to play in his second all-star game, held in February of 1984 at New Jersey's Brendan Byrne Arena. A relieved Sather had noted the change in his former No. 1 draft pick. "Grant had an off-year last year," Sather told reporters in something of an understatement. "This year he got off to a great start and played well all the way through."

The psychological impact of Grant's comeback was immediate on the young Oilers, freeing them to step up their game. As Hall of Fame goalie Ken Dryden wrote in *The Game*, "[A goalie's] job is to stop pucks. . . . Well, yeah, that's part of it. But you know what else it is? . . . You're trying to deliver a message to your team that things are OK back here. This end of the ice is pretty well cared for. You take it now and go. Go! Feel the freedom you need in order to be that dynamic, creative, offensive player and go out and score. . . . That was my job. And it was to try to deliver a feeling."

Edmonton's 1983–84 campaign was the most successful regular season for any NHL club in seven years, and as the Oilers cruised to a record season, Grant also studied the artistry of the Great One on and off the ice. That season, Gretzky scored 87 goals with 205 points, just behind his best year in 1981–82 (92 goals and 212 points), but still a year unlikely to be matched in the modern NHL.

Grant:
We had the pleasure of watching Gretz from the beginning, so it was fun to see it all culminate. Everybody knew he's the guy. You couldn't ask for a nicer guy to be around. Every night there was a circus around him. You felt bad for him, because he never got a breather. But he did it all with a smile, and you'd just sit there in awe and watch him deal with it every single day. It literally was every day.

Everybody knows how great a hockey player he is. But people don't realize what a great person he is. The young guys, when they first came in,

Gretz had them stay with him instead of staying at a hotel. Take them for dinner, feed them, look after them. It was more about making the young guys feel like they were part of the team. They were comfortable, and it was part of what made us good. It could be a little bit intimidating for a new guy walking in to see Gretz and Coff and Mess, but everybody got made to feel like they were part of it right out of the gate. I think that's what kept us at the top of everything: everybody felt like they fit right away, so there's no transition period. Everybody that came in fit. If they didn't fit, then we got rid of them.

It was like a big group of kids having fun. Most of us weren't married by then [11, in fact], so we had a lot of time to hang out together.

Even when we weren't playing well we were having more fun than everybody else. And Slats let us have fun. You had fun at practice, because he made practices fun, so the guys wanted to be there. We probably drove the trainers nuts, because the guys would stay on the ice and practise when they wanted to get everything packed up. Then the guys would want to go play ping-pong afterwards. So you're there until three or four in the afternoon, and there'd be 10 or 12 guys still there.

We just assumed everywhere was like that. That was the biggest news: I just thought that's the way that National Hockey League works. Then other teams would come in and they'd be like, "Woo! You've got a pretty good squad." And we would say, "Yeah, I guess we do."

But fun wasn't enough, and Gretzky and the Oilers had the scars to prove that regular-season dominance does not guarantee playoff success. They would be defined by the Stanley Cups they won, and to achieve that goal they would need a stellar goalie who could last the heated four rounds needed to win them. Sather had his two viable options in net, but when the playoffs began, he handed the baton to Fuhr. Grant's 11–4 mark with a .903 save percentage in the 1984 post-season was the start of his glorious run as a "money" goalie. Much like his Islanders counterpart Billy Smith—who routinely split regular-season games with Glenn "Chico" Resch and Rollie Melanson, but was irreplaceable come playoff time—Grant took the permanent job in the post-season and ran with it. After a relaxing three-game sweep of the Winnipeg Jets in the Smythe semis, Fuhr was singled out for praise in the 4–1 victory in Game 3. "The Jets made our team work for everything," Sather told reporters. "If there was one difference in the series, it was Grant Fuhr. He made tremendous saves when we needed them."

There were more pitfalls ahead, however. In the second installment of the Battle of Alberta, the stubborn Calgary Flames, led by Paul Reinhart, pushed the Oilers to seven games in the Smythe Division final. Grant and Moog actually shared the goaltending duties in Game 7 as Edmonton peppered 44 shots on Flames goalie Rejean Lemelin, but the Oilers still needed to score the final four goals (two in 58 seconds) to carve out the 7–4 win. Next, a bruised shoulder that Grant suffered in Game 2 of the Campbell finals against the North Stars led to Moog starting the 8–5 win in Game 3. But Grant was again back in the Oilers net for the clinching 3–1 Game 4 victory and another Campbell Bowl win for Edmonton as they swept the outmatched Minnesotans. Going into the Finals rematch with the Islanders, Grant seemed the natural choice for the Game 1 start. The thinking was that his first taste of the Cup pressure would give the Oilers extra energy—and perhaps give the Isles fits. Grant was ready.

Grant:

I'd been like a cheerleader the year before, when Andy played the final against the Islanders. It's not what you want: you want to be the one playing. But that was the place I had drawn. That was my role. I'm not sure how ready I would have been to play in that atmosphere after the year I'd had in 1982–83. My confidence was shaky that season. You can't win at that level of the playoffs if you're not certain. Your teammates can see it—and the other team can see it, too.

But with his confidence restored in 1984 it was full steam ahead, and Grant happily anticipated the challenge of another showdown with Billy Smith, his hated rival in the Islanders net. As Game 1 dawned, however, there remained critics who pointed out flaws in the Oilers as a team, and in their acrobatic goalie. Conventional hockey wisdom had always held that defence wins championships; in 1983–84, the high-octane Oilers were seeking to prove that mantra a fallacy. Most of those critics assembled for Game 1 in Uniondale assumed that if the Oilers were to win over Al Arbour's fanatically disciplined team, it could only be by using their vaunted scoring to overwhelm the Isles. After all, Glen Sather's crew couldn't play defence, and was totally dependent on Gretzky's line to power the team. As proof, critics pointed to the five losses in a row the Oilers had racked up (including an 11–0 loss Grant suffered at the hands of the Hartford Whalers on February 12) when both Gretzky and Jari Kurri were out of the lineup.

There were also questions specifically about Grant, who was said to need the safety net of his team's great offence to bolster him. He could give up soft goals and still win in the regular season, according to his critics, but what would happen in a low-scoring game when that safety net was pulled away and every goal mattered? As Kirk McLean, Vancouver's star goalie of the 1990s, would later note, "It is pretty tough for a goalie when you look at it. You're always the last line of defence. If you let a goal in, you can't go to the bench and hide between the guys or anything."

Grant was about to set all that thinking on its ear. The learning curve from his stumbles in 1982–83 was set to pay off as he nervously waited for the end of the national anthem before Game 1. Once the puck dropped, the New York Islanders saw a new man. Sather's decision to go with No. 31 was rewarded with what is considered perhaps the most important Oiler victory ever—a tension-filled 1–0 road shutout before 15,861 at the Nassau County Coliseum, with the supposedly sieve-like Oilers winning in a most atypical fashion.

Grant:

That game was so much fun to play. We knew going into the Island that we had to be very good in Game 1. Especially on defence. We wanted to show them that we could play any style they wanted, and we'd still win. It was just one of those nights where you're comfortable: the shots you don't see hit you, and they hit the middle of your body, and you just know it's going to be one of those nights. Between periods in the dressing room we knew we had a chance. We'd learned from the year before: they'd kind of run over us the year before, where we got a little caught up in the emotion. The next year, we just played.

I think that was the biggest difference. We saw how they dealt with it, and we figured if we did the same thing, then we had a good chance. Everything just happened to fall into place at one time. Once we had won that game we realized that we were good enough to play with them. Any style that we wanted to play we could play.

Kelly Hrudey, who was the Islanders' third goalie, was left grudgingly admiring Grant's performance. "He was spectacular," says Hrudey. "Our guys had so many good chances that night and he just turned them all away."

Grant's many thieving saves on Islander forwards left reporters and fans grasping for superlatives too. "One of those stops—a left-pad split save of a Bryan Trottier 15-footer from dead in front, followed by a stacked-pad smothering of Trottier's rebound—was easily the best and most important of the series," wrote Jack Falla in *Sports Illustrated.* "The key to the Islanders' previous mastery of the Oilers had been New York's ability to take a lead and then close the door." An Associated Press game story described how Grant "orchestrated the victory with cat-like quickness." Sather could only smile. "He was as good as Billy Smith tonight. If we get goaltending like that (the rest of the series), we'll be in good shape."

"What struck me was how relaxed he was," said Smith, who'd go on to make the Hall of Fame 10 years before Grant. "He was very different than me. I showed up at the rink with a burr up my ass. We were very different personalities, but he was a helluva competitor."

When the game ended it was the first time the Islanders had ever been shut out in the Stanley Cup Finals. Their nine-game Finals win streak was ended by Grant's brilliant performance, and his mastery set the tone for the sea change to follow in the series. Considering how rare shutouts were in an era of all-out offence, many believe that, for all the great games to come, Game 1 was likely Grant's definitive star performance. With a skeptical world-wide audience tuning in to see if Gretzky's guys were all show and no go for a second consecutive year, the mental block lifted by that win was huge.

But if the Oilers thought they were home and cooled out against a defeated Islanders team, Game 2 brought a sharp comeuppance.

Grant:

We go to Game 2 on Long Island. We're feeling pretty good. I'm feeling pretty good. We're told that we're supposed to leave [Islander forward]

Clark Gillies alone. We didn't want to wake him up. So what do we
do? We run him in the first shift. We lose 6–1, Gillies scores three
goals, Bryan Trottier gets two. And right then we figured out that for
as hard as we worked the first night in Game 1, we didn't work half as
hard the second night. And that they're still a really good hockey team.
Losing 6–1 was probably the best thing that could have happened
to us, because we realized we had to be that much better, that much
more focused.

Back before the home fans in Game 3 at a delirious Northlands
Coliseum, the results of that realization were not immediately
apparent. Clark Gillies gave New York the first goal, beating Grant
just 1:32 into the contest. Gillies' second goal of the game on the
power play gave New York a 2–1 lead early in the second period.
That lasted until 8:28 of the second, when a signature Mark Messier
goal—his brilliant deke on Isles defenceman Gord Dineen sent
him in alone on Smith for the score—tied the game.

A 40-shot barrage from the Oilers forced Arbour to pull Billy
Smith for the first of two straight games. Meanwhile, Grant was
riding high with 23 saves on 25 shots late in the third—until his
giddiness was cut short as he wandered along the boards to the
right of his net.

Grant:

Game 3, we get the nice lead, and then I decided I should handle the
puck in the corner to my right. I was going out to play the puck, and Patty
LaFontaine was coming to check me, and I forgot where the defenceman
was. He ended up drilling me. I hit dead on the boards with the point at
my shoulder. I jammed the joint so badly that I couldn't lift my arm up for
about two weeks. That injury would hurt for a long time.

Moog took over again with seven minutes left in Game 3, which Edmonton won 7–2. Then he backstopped another 7–2 win, and finally the 5–2 victory that clinched the first Stanley Cup for the Oilers over an exhausted Islanders squad playing its fifth straight Cup final. Though Moog closed out the series, and Messier's turn-around goal in Game 3 propelled "Moose" toward a Conn Smythe Trophy, no one forgot that Grant's first Stanley Cup final game—and first playoff shutout—was an early sign that the Oilers could play stingy and also had a big-name goalie of their own.

The Oilers became the first former WHA team to win the Cup, and the first team west of Chicago to win the Stanley Cup since the WCHL's Victoria Cougars in 1925. For the city of Edmonton, which was already in the midst of five consecutive Grey Cup wins by the CFL's Eskimos, a Stanley Cup was an even greater celebration. It was a great time to be a hero in the city.

Grant:

Edmonton's a special sports city. People care. It's 365 days a year. Just because you've left the rink doesn't mean it's ended. You go to the grocery store, people still care. You go to a bar, people still care. Everybody cares and they care 24/7. It's also a great atmosphere to play in. There are expectations after what we did and the Eskimos did. Some of the kids that are playing there now are having a hard time with that.

No one partied harder or longer with the fans of Edmonton than the young men who made up the remarkable Edmonton Oilers.

Grant:

We probably ran for half a dozen, maybe seven days. I was actually pretty good about functioning on two or three hours of sleep by then. Everywhere you went you took the Cup and everywhere was a party. Everywhere you went in the city you couldn't pay for anything, and it ran like that for a long time. It ran like that for probably a month. Barry T's was the big place in Edmonton at that time. The American Bar over in the West End. There was a certain place to go every night. You could show up there thinking you wouldn't run into anybody and there were always six or seven guys there you knew. Usually teammates.

[Before the Stanley Cup] you're getting extra hours in practice to try and figure it out, so you really don't have time to be out socializing, because you know the work the next day is going to be hard. More and more people are coming around, though, trying to get close to you. But for the most part life was pretty quiet before the Cup in '84. I was running around like a normal teenager would, but nothing outrageous. Then, in 1984 you started to see the new people arrive on the scene, the girls got prettier, all that fun stuff.

The Cup win also brought out more than the usual fans. Amidst the legions coming to say hello to the conquering hero was a character who emerged one late evening from the dim lights of the nightclub. The black man, in his late 30s, was introduced to Grant as the netminder relaxed with friends in the club. For Grant, whose present was so promising, the introduction brought him face to face with his past. The stranger intimated that he was the natural father Grant had never known.

Grant:

We just happened to be sitting there. It was a normal place where we'd gone lots. Most people knew we were there. Somebody else brought him up and had introduced him as my natural father. . . . In that kind of situation, you never know for sure whether it is or it isn't the real person, and I didn't really worry about it that much at that time. So, we spent about 10 minutes talking to him, same as you would with anybody that walks up and meets you at the bar.

My mom had explained years before about what had happened with my parents. They were young. I think he was 17, and my natural mom would have been 15. It wasn't going to work anyway at their ages. I mean, if it was my natural father, great. If it's not then that's fine too. My mom and dad were still my parents, always had been. Always would be. I have never heard or seen the guy since, so I have no idea what happened to him. As a father myself, I know how hard it would be to stay away. That would be tough. But at the same time, you don't know if it would have changed anything or not. I never really worried about it. I'd managed to complicate life enough by that point.

Grant being on his own created challenges stemming from having a lot of money at such a young age. "He decided he was going to paint his house out in Spruce Grove with his buddies," recalls Marty McSorley. "They got it half done, and they just left it. I was over at the house one day and I teased him because I looked out the window to the back yard and the grass was so long it looked like a zoo. There must be lions and tigers out there."

There was also a story that Grant once tried to sell a car he had been leasing. Ominously, Sather also began hearing about outstanding bills at local bars, to the tune of $3,500.

In a scathing interview with *Sports Illustrated* years later, Sather would recall the kid who couldn't say no. "He was running a tab, and everybody in town was using it. He didn't know what he was getting into," Sather told the magazine. "Grant's not exactly a wizard when it comes to finances." In 1984, Sather became Fuhr's unofficial financial manager. When he learned Grant was paying some $1,200 a month in rent, he suggested that the Oilers buy the house for him and arrange mortgaging so Grant could both build equity and lower his monthly payments.

In December of that same year, the Oilers reportedly advanced

Grant $91,890 toward the purchase and held a lien against the house. They also directly handled Fuhr's monthly mortgage and utility payments for him. "He's had his utilities shut off, because he never pays them," Sather told *SI*. "So what I have done is watch his money. I tell him what he can and cannot do. I also charge him $100 a month for accounting. And interest [on the house loan]. Why do we manage his money? Why do we have to have a lien against him? Because he can't take care of his money. The problems Grant's got come from a kid that is dumb."

Sather's comments stung Grant. He didn't help matters by telling the magazine how he'd run up a huge debt at a video store: "When my clothes were dirty, I just threw them in the closet and went out and bought something else, Some of the (rented videos) ended up in the closet under the dirty clothes."

Grant:

I wasn't a dumb kid. I was a kid having fun and doing dumb things. We do things when we're younger, that's how we learn. I just had a little more money than most kids my age. And people knew who I was from the Oilers. I couldn't spend it all. I used to go out with a lot of the guys from the Eskimos. Both teams liked each other. So that was a good thing too. Slats might not have seen it that way some days. At the time I didn't care what anyone said. I was having fun. But I don't regret those days: I wouldn't take them back for anything.

In the years ahead, Grant would learn just how much more complicated his life could be.

GAME 4

Grant Fuhr sat beside his father's bed, talking hockey as the two men had done since Grant was a boy. Bob might not have been Grant's natural father, but the pair had bonded at a deep level through their mutual interest in sports. They talked late into the night, hours after Grant had backstopped the Oilers to a 7–3 win over the Vancouver Canucks in Game 1 of the 1986 playoffs. As always, Bob Fuhr had been watching on TV. This time was different, however; Bob watched from his bed at the Misericordia Community Hospital in Edmonton. While the Oilers had been prohibitive favourites to beat Vancouver in the contest, the Canucks had narrowed the Edmonton lead to 3–2 heading into the final period. Grant allowed just one more goal on 13 Canuck shots, and the vaunted Edmonton offence stretched its lead against Richard Brodeur in the Vancouver net. Had it not been for Brodeur's heroics, the Oilers might have reached double figures in goals.

Seeing Grant and his team pull away in the third was a pleasure for the former teacher-turned-insurance salesman. Having Grant come straight from the victory at Northlands to see him afterwards was even more pleasing. Sports were how father and son had communicated almost from the day Grant could carry on a conversation.

Whether in the car on the way to a practice or at the family dinner table, talking sports, going over the details of another win for one of Grant's teams, had kept the two in touch. It had been the perfect formula for a father looking to connect with his adoptive son.

Grant:

He used to play all kind of sports when he was younger, and he kept on playing when I was growing up. He never had to force it on me. When I saw him play hockey, I wanted to play hockey. When he took me out golfing, I wanted to play golf. We would talk about it as we watched on TV. It just came naturally to do it.

Suddenly, that close bond was threatened by Bob's illness. At 51 years old, the elder Fuhr had rarely been sick in his life prior to the spring of 1986. Now he was stuck in a hospital bed watching his son, arguably the best goalie in the world, start the Oilers on the path to what everyone hoped would be their third straight Stanley Cup. Grant knew the prognosis was not good, but there was no sense of crisis in the room that night.

Grant:

What happened was my father ran over his toes with the lawnmower. And he ran over his toes because he was mowing the lawn in his slippers. For the life of me I don't know why he did that, but he always did. We asked him not to, but he didn't listen. So he went to get his toes sewn back on, and they did some blood work. That's when they discovered the cancer. He went into the hospital—that would have been one of the first times mowing the lawn that year—so in April, give or take. He went in two weeks before we played the Canucks in the first round.

He actually watched the game that night. So that was good. We talked about how the game went and our chances at getting another Cup. He was pretty sure we were going to win another. We sat up chatting all night till four in the morning. We all thought he'd be around for awhile yet.

Then he passed away when I was at practice the next morning. I think that might have been the hardest shock—that he went so quickly. Got things off on the wrong foot for the playoffs. That summer was probably the turning point where things got a little out of hand in my life. That month kind of turned everything bad. For about two-and-a-half months after that everything ran amuck.

The poet Diana Der-Hovanessian wrote, "When you father dies, say the Indians, he comes back as the thunder." For a grieving Grant, thunder and storms would run roughshod through his life in the wake of his father's sudden passing.

Following the Oilers' first Stanley Cup triumph in 1984, the hockey world had been expecting the dawn of a new era of sustained excellence from Gretzky and Co. The Islanders and Canadiens had owned the Stanley Cup for the previous eight years, creating dynasties as they each won four consecutive Cups. Now it was expected that Wayne Gretzky's prodigious Oilers would follow suit with four (or more) in a row of their own. And why not? Like 22-year-old Grant, the Oilers' core was just entering its prime. Gretzky, Messier, Kurri, Coffey and Fuhr were the envy of hockey. There was the possibility of as many as a decade of championship runs if everyone stayed healthy—and if distressed owner Peter Pocklington could afford to pay the splendid squad in the face of a declining Canadian dollar and his own fiscal nightmares. Still, the team needed to stay focused.

As his players emerged from the haze of that inaugural summer of Cup celebration, general manager Glen Sather had a message for his team, a dazzling assembly of skill and speed that some predicted would be the "Greatest Team Ever."

Grant:

We ran hard for awhile that summer, soaking it in, getting all the congratu-
lations, taking the Cup all over the place. Then Slats reeled us all in. He
reminded us that winning one was great. But it's even harder to repeat.
We thought we knew what he meant. But we discovered over the next
couple of years that it was a lot harder than we thought. We got everyone's
best game every night. And there were no excuses in Edmonton for
anything but the best.

For Grant, who'd been forced to watch the 1984 Cup clincher
against the Islanders from the bench with a bad shoulder, repeating
as Cup champion was about more than another ring. It was also
about regaining his role as No. 1 goalie for the key games that would
define the Oilers legacy. He had proven his mettle in the Game 1
shutout of the Islanders, but having been denied the chance to start
in net for the deciding game, Grant was determined to use 1984–85
as a springboard to perfection.

Grant:

It was great watching us win the Cup against the Islanders. But it also
felt like I should have been the one out there. Andy played great; you
were happy for him. But you grow up as a kid dreaming of being the
guy on the ice with the Stanley Cup—not the guy watching from the
press box. Anytime I needed a boost that season I just had to remember
that feeling.

The 1984–85 season proved a fitting one in which to remember.
In April, the Oilers finished atop the Campbell Conference with
109 points. But every one of them was hard-won.

Grant:

Winning the first year was hard. Winning the second year was harder. You played 82 playoff games, because everybody wants to beat the defending Stanley Cup champion. Then you get appreciation for what the Islanders had gone through. Now, there's no easy games. It doesn't matter how many points you are ahead of the team behind you; every game's hard, the whole year. But we enjoyed the games like that. Everybody tried to play the hardest. It's fun to repeat: you enjoy it more.

Coming back strong from his shoulder issue, No. 31 posted a 26–8–7 mark with one shutout on the season. Grant's numbers were actually better than the season before (a 3.87 GAA and .884 save percentage), and although he incurred yet another separated shoulder injury in February, he still managed to start a career-high 46 games in tandem with Andy Moog.

Grant:

We never knew who was starting until the morning of the game. You could play four in a row, you could play eight in a row—but at the end of the day, over the course of 80 games, you'd be starting 39, 41 games. It would always work out to be close, but there was no set schedule to it, so you had to prepare like you were going to play every day. Actually, it was great, because it made you ready to play. Even if a guy got pulled, you were still ready because you had prepared. Sometimes [Sather] wouldn't tell you until after the morning skate. So you worked just as hard.

Later, I went from Andy as partner to Bill Ranford—the same thing. Competition.

Despite the challenges of the regular season, however, the 1985 post-season proved less of a struggle than the previous year's conquest. Edmonton went a sparkling 15–3 with Grant getting credit for every win (the first round was still a best-of-five). He performed steadily with a 3.10 GAA and .895 save percentage in the playoffs as the Oilers rolled through Los Angeles, Winnipeg and Chicago. But his best play was saved for the Cup finals, where he outshone the Vezina/Jennings Trophy tandem of Pelle Lindbergh and Bob Froese from Philadelphia, allowing 13 goals in 5 games compared to 21 allowed by the Flyers goalies. Grant also became the first goalie to stop two penalty shots in one series, turning back efforts in Games 3 and 4. While many goalies hated the pressure of that moment, Grant relished the one-on-one challenge of a penalty shot.

Grant:

It's a battle of patience: the longer you can wait the harder it is for the forward. I always think that I have the advantage because I can move last, if I want. You can also force them to where you want them to go if you can be patient enough. The player has a split second usually to see what space he wants to shoot at. So you just make sure that he sees the space that you want him to see. That's what makes your glove hand best. If I can get you to look at my glove hand and shoot there—I've got an advantage. You go into my strength. The harder shot to stop is the one right at you. It's hard to stand there and wait. It's why the five hole is such a hard save: you want to move. I would have liked the shoot-out. It would have been fun for me.

So great was the Oilers' margin of victory that spring, Grant's heroics might not have meant the same degree of difference between victory and defeat as they had in 1984. His teammates supplied him with 98 goals—an average of 5.44 per game—the greatest offensive post-season in NHL history. Wayne Gretzky alone accumulated a record 17 goals and 47 points on the way to his first Conn Smythe Trophy. But Grant was still stellar: aside from an 8–6 beating at the hands of Chicago in Game 4 of the Campbell final, Grant never left the Oilers in difficult situations, forced them to play catch-up or suffer an off game.

The most telling indicator of Grant's worth instead came from the NHL general managers who vote on the Vezina Trophy; they saw his work—not Moog's—as more essential to the Oilers' success. Grant finished third in the voting, a finalist for the award for the first time since his rookie year. Everything was looking up for Edmonton and pointing toward a sure third straight championship en route to cementing the high-flying Oilers as hockey's newest dynasty.

For Grant, life was a banquet—and he and roommate Kevin McClelland enjoyed the meal. It wasn't just a metaphor: McClelland marvelled at Grant's unique dietary approach. "Fuhrsie's a little overweight," he told filmmaker Bob McKeown for his documentary *The Boys Are Back*. "He's 195 [pounds]. He's supposed to be 182. He eats six cheeseburgers all the time . . . I don't understand the guy."

If possible, things seemed to come even easier to the two-time defending champions during the 1985–86 season. Darlings of the media in general, and heroes to broadcasters like Peter Gzowski (who lionized their attractive version of offensive hockey), the Oilers were extolled everywhere they went. "The game they play is the game all of us played," gushed Gzowski, who grew up on the rinks of Guelph, Ontario. "But the game of our lives is the business of theirs, and they are a long way from Dickson Park [in Guelph]."

It seemed that the merry-go-round of titles and fun would never stop spinning. Trashing the competition on the way to a first-overall finish with 119 points in 1985–86, the Oilers saw Gretzky break his own assists and points records for the last time, while

Paul Coffey piled up an astounding 48 goals to break Bobby Orr's record for goals by a defenceman in a season (another record likely never to be approached again, let alone matched). And though Grant played just 40 games to Moog's 47, and his GAA was again inferior to his partner's (3.90 to Moog's 3.69), Grant owned a slightly better save percentage.

The first round of the 1986 playoffs was a cakewalk, with the Oilers going easy on the mediocre Canucks by "only" beating them 7–3, 5–1, and 5–1 in a sweep. But compared to the 13–0 embarrassment they'd laid on Vancouver earlier that year, the playoff dusting was child's play.

In the midst of the anticipation for a third Cup, however, there were stories of the distractions dogging the Oilers: the internal battles over contracts for their stars, who seemed to be falling behind the league's payment standards; the fast-and-loose attitude on the ice toward a team concept. Within the Oilers' management, there was doubt about the team's commitment, doubts that would surface a year later when John Muckler, the Oilers' co-coach, noted, "I don't think we were a team [in 1986]. The Stanley Cup is a team championship. The team that wins the Cup is the best team, not necessarily the team with the most talent."

On top of the controversies swirling around him and his team, there was also the personal heartache in store for Grant both on and off the ice. The advanced cancer diagnosis came in on Bob Fuhr just as the 1985–86 season wound down, and life took on a new urgency. Suddenly, time was of the essence for father and son. In the midst of preparing for the playoffs, Grant would spend as much time as he could with the man who'd accepted him into his heart as his own son in 1962. "At least I got to see him after the game. It's been coming for a while," a sombre Grant told Cam Cole of the *Edmonton Journal*.

For a numbed Grant, it seemed the best way to get through the shock of his father's passing was to submerge himself in hockey. He asked to play in Game 2 against the Canucks and was initially granted the okay from Moog to do so; then plans changed. Moog would play Game 2, and after spending much of the day with his mourning family, Grant instead watched from the bench as Moog and the Oilers cruised to a 5–1 win.

Grant:

I did want to play. It would have been easier. Less thinking. And as a tribute to my dad. But they went in there without me. It wasn't to be.

Two days later in Vancouver, Grant was back in the Oilers net. His team made it easy for the grieving goalie, outshooting the Canucks 41–22 in a repeat 5–1 score. In front of an apathetic crowd of 7,854 at the Pacific Coliseum, Grant paid tribute to his dad in the way he knew best. Only a third-period goal from Thomas Gradin denied him the shutout. "I wanted [the shutout] for my dad," Grant told reporters afterwards. "I'll get one though . . . somewhere, somehow. It's only a matter of time." Grant summed up his team's total domination of the Canucks, quipping, "Without Brodeur playing so well, maybe we would have won 10–1. He was the only reason it stayed respectable."

For Grant, the loss was not just that of a father but of a competitive partner and sporting comrade. Bob had not only introduced his son to hockey and baseball, he'd also taught Grant to play golf, starting a lifelong passion for the game in the young man. As a junior player in Victoria, Grant had found the rainy, temperate climate of Vancouver Island perfect for his new hobby, and he was able to play year-round and quickly bring down his handicap. From then on, the sport became his refuge. By the time he was an established NHL star, he would sometimes play 36 holes on an off-day. As Marty McSorley noted, "It was his place to relax. If he wanted to play a couple of rounds between games, no one bothered him about it."

Grant:

After my dad had introduced me to the game, I started playing lots of golf. I got to play some fabulous golf courses in Victoria. We were able to play in Gorge Vale a lot. We played at a place called Royal Colwood, which I think is probably one of the top 10 or 15 golf courses in Canada. Cedar Hills was another good golf course, took good care of us. It was a good place to start learning how to golf. From there it just took off. When they wouldn't let me play other sports, golf was a place I could go to stay competitive, be sharp.

Hand-eye coordination is similar, except you're not trying to catch anything. The focus is the same. It's a four-hour adventure. You've got to stay focused. Your body is getting a break, but your mind's working. It's a different thought process than playing hockey, because it's not a reaction sport, so you're not burning yourself out.

Regardless of the sport, it was Bob, an optimist by nature, who had played a major role in Grant's development as a pro athlete. Grant's mother, Betty, saw their bond. "He and his dad were very close," she told *SI*. "They both were very sports-minded." Betty, who died in 2000, also saw that her husband had concerns about the carefree Grant being chewed up in the harsh world of pro sports. "Robert was a little concerned. . . . He knew the dedication, the sacrifice it took to play in the NHL as a goalie, and Grant was always such a happy-go-lucky child."

When Grant started ascending the ranks of youth hockey, he received some excellent advice from his adoptive father.

Grant:

He told me not to worry. He told me to have fun and enjoy life. He told me that as soon as hockey became a job, to leave it alone. He also played a lot and he coached me a lot as a kid. We kind of worked hand in hand. There was no dictation that you had to do it. I mean, you see a lot of parents now that are critical about their kids that are playing, and I noticed that the last few years when I was coaching minor hockey. He would never be critical. He would ask me how I thought I played and leave it alone until the next day. Then he might make a comment somewhere along the way. Never criticized anything, just "Would you think it'd be better if you did this and you did that?" to leave you thinking about it.

You played because you loved doing it. Now, you're seeing some kids that are being told they have to do it. The parents think you have to do it 24/7, 12 months of the year. It's not like that. If I had done it 24/7 I would have been tired by the time I was 20 and probably would have never turned pro. My dad shielded me from that. The fact that I got to get away, play baseball, do different things, play football for a little bit, my dad helped with that. He didn't put pressure on me. More than anything, he was someone I could bounce things off of.

Grant was hoping to memorialize his father with another Stanley Cup in the spring of 1986. The Oilers' dream of a third straight championship hinged on a Smythe Division final matchup against the rival Calgary Flames in another Battle of Alberta classic. While Calgary had finished 30 points behind the Oilers, they were always a formidable foe when the clubs met in the provincial "death match."

Grant:

We played Calgary, which was, as always, fun. A see-saw battle. Obviously, our best rivalry was with the Flames, the Battle of Alberta. Al MacInnis came out the same year as I did. He went to Calgary while I was selected by Edmonton. He really could shoot the puck as well. He was a little wild his first couple of years, so everything was a little higher up. They had some good players: Lanny McDonald could still shoot the puck. Hakan Loob was a good hockey player. Kent Nilsson. Doug Gilmour was always in your face, always talking to you—we had fun with that. Theo Fleury was fun to play against, because he was as competitive as could be. John Tonelli, because of the Islanders' run, and then ending up in Calgary—it was fun to play against him. Joel Otto was a challenge in front of the net. Then there was Vernie [Mike Vernon] at the other end. We'd played each other going back to our days in minor hockey in Alberta.

It was all making to be a great series for us. And then it ended on a crushing note, which everybody remembers. And if you don't, they show it on TV all the time. So that was kind of a gloomy end to a gloomy month.

Ah yes, the "own goal."

After a tense six games of the Campbell Conference semi-final, the Oilers and Flames came to a Game 7 showdown on April 30. Edmonton always appeared to be playing from behind in the series as Calgary coach Bob Johnson threw a blanket over the Oilers' power offence. Once more, Calgary gained a 2–0 lead only to see Edmonton come back to tie the contest. The Oilers seemed to be building momentum as the second period came to a close in a raucous Northlands Coliseum. Then, five minutes into the third period, disaster struck. Rookie defenceman Steve Smith's cross-ice pass from behind his own net bounced off the back of Fuhr's left pad and into the Oiler net for what would eventually prove to be the winning goal. Calgary's Perry Berezan, who was credited with the goal off his dump-in pass, was on the Flames bench. "I never saw the goal," Berezan admitted later. "I was just sitting down and I heard this noise."

As Grant stood, stunned, looking at the puck behind him, Smith collapsed to the ice and the Northlands crowd groaned. There was 14:46 remaining, but the Oilers never recovered, and the Flames went on to meet Montreal in the 1986 Cup Final. While Grant was one of the least culpable in the blame game after the series, he had nonetheless been out-duelled for arguably the first time in his play-off career as his old rival Mike Vernon stole the show.

Things were about to get worse. Within days of the Oilers' elimination, *Sports Illustrated* came out with a blockbuster report claiming that five Oilers were using cocaine. Rumours suggested that Grant was one. The weight of the *SI* story, the loss to Calgary and his dad's passing culminated in a turbulent time in both Grant's professional and personal lives. His use of recreational drugs—often rumoured in the press and leaked to Oilers management—was taking a toll.

Grant:
It had gone on like that for about three years. But I had been able to keep that separate from the hockey. As long as they didn't blend it was okay. Then in the summer of '86, the end of that year was kind of a real crashing halt for me. Things took a turn for the worse. I hadn't prepared for it whatsoever. We got the lovely Steve Smith goal, and Dad had passed away two weeks before that. It was a hard summer.

We definitely partied too much. But it wasn't so much for the fun part of it. For the longest time there had been no harm, no foul in what we did. But '86 was probably the turning point, where things got a little out of hand. Things blended together. That month kind of turned everything bad.

Grant sought the privacy of Edmonton nights to work out his pain and frustration from a year gone wrong.

Grant:

I could hide with the best of them. It was the one thing that I knew how to do very well. I could blend into little neighbourhood bars and stuff where nobody would know who I was, even in Edmonton. Nobody would know where to look.

Marty McSorley had an up-close view of how Grant's life was spiralling out of control. "Grant never led socially," McSorley recalls. "If you said to him at 11 o'clock, let's go home, he'd go home. But if you said let's go to another party, he'd go with you. He never said, 'Let's go do this, or let's go do that.' He was a very good guy. Even when there were some issues during his career he wasn't a hell raiser. He was not a guy to look for trouble. He would follow somebody's lead. And it was sad because you'd like to think that the people cared enough about him to lead him in the right direction. But that didn't happen."

Grant's marriage to his wife, Corrine (whom he'd married in 1983), was also showing the stress of balancing an NHL career, a family and a raging nightlife. Over the next year, it would come apart.

Grant:

It had gotten a little out of control, but we enjoyed each other's company too. We had two daughters at that time, so all that being thrown into the big picture was just something more to juggle along with everything else. We just decided we were going different directions and wanted to stay friends. And to this day we're still friends, which is good.

At the conclusion of that bruising summer, Grant's solution to his distress was to bury himself in hockey, the only safe haven he knew. After a long time submerged in his own private world, he found salvation in the sport he'd known since boyhood, and the men with whom he shared the Oilers dressing room.

Grant:

About September that year, I kind of re-grasped the world again. And that year was probably the best year I had in hockey. The Rendez-vous series, Canada Cup and the Stanley Cup all in one year. The only thing that I cared about was the hockey. I'm pretty good at focusing on one thing: we still went out a bit, but hockey was everything. In '87 we worried about one thing and one thing only: hockey.

Grant wasn't the only one looking for vindication in 1986–87. The entire Edmonton organization was seeking redemption after the previous season's disastrous end against Calgary. In what was a put-up-or-shut-up situation for the Oilers, Gretzky and crew delivered a season for the ages—one that began with Grant's greatest role in his country's uniform.

GAME 5

A fter the debacle of Steve Smith's "own goal" in 1986 had wrecked the Oilers' dream of four consecutive Cups, the media and fans were pitiless about the distractions surrounding their team. Grant was still coping poorly with the sudden passing of his father and its effects on his life. Was Wayne Gretzky spending too much time in Hollywood with his new girlfriend, actress Janet Jones? Paul Coffey, Andy Moog and Grant were all in contract negotiations with the Oilers, rancorous talks that threatened to disperse the core of the team.

In the wake of all these mini dramas, general manager and head coach Glen Sather needed to impose order—and quickly—upon his young players before things spun out of control. After Edmonton's run-and-gun style was exploited by the Calgary Flames' aggressive forecheck in the 1986 playoffs, Sather made the decision to change gears. He implemented the stingy checking style of co-coach John Muckler throughout the 1986–87 season. This more conservative approach was partly necessitated by high-scoring defenceman Paul Coffey missing 21 games to injury—and partly by Sather's criticism of Coffey's play in 1986 as defensively irresponsible. As a result, Sather cut back on the Norris winner's ice time, sowing seeds of discontent that led to the first of many Oiler defections (Coffey was dealt to Pittsburgh in late 1987).

While the forwards and defencemen were reined in, Sather declared it business as usual for Edmonton in goal, with Grant and Moog splitting the duties once again. For the second consecutive year Moog appeared in more games, 46 to Grant's 44. This time, while Grant again had a lower GAA, he also had the lower winning percentage at 22–13–3, his worst record since 1982–83. That said, the duo cut the Oilers' goals-allowed total from 310 to 284, a new franchise low. (While no one acknowledged it at the time, it was to be the final full year for the Fuhr/Moog tandem as Moog sought a No. 1 position somewhere else in the league.) Grant found some peace between the pipes. "The one place he was comfortable was in the net," recalls Marty McSorley. "I don't know that he was totally comfortable in other situations in the locker room. He wasn't always confident in there, and he'd say weird things. And you'd go, 'C'mon Fuhrsie . . .' Not in a bad way, but he didn't always know how to react to it. I never saw him have a mean moment. I saw him be disappointed, a lot of the time with himself because he wanted to win. But I never saw a mean moment with a teammate or a fan."

It was more than NHL shooters who'd be challenging Grant in the net that season. With the Canada Cup on the horizon in September 1987, Grant got an early glimpse of the vaunted Soviet machine in February of that year. An NHL all-star team took on the USSR in a pair of games in Quebec City as part of the Rendez-vous series, the pet project of Quebec Nordiques owner Marcel Aubut. In the first game, Grant turned away 24 of 27 shots as the NHLers triumphed 4–3. The Soviets reversed the tables on Grant and his teammates in Game 2, however, winning 5–3. Used to the storm-the-walls style of the NHL, Grant now had to accommodate himself to the patient patterns of Viktor Tikhonov's Soviets, patterns that resembled soccer strategy as much as hockey.

Grant:

You can't be all helter-skelter and throw yourself all over the place. You have to have a little more patience. It's completely different than anything you know. So that took a little bit of learning. At the same time you're learning by fire. At that level, with the whole country watching, you couldn't be bad while you learn. It was a real challenge.

Back for the stretch run with the Oilers after facing the Soviets, Grant benefited both from having raised his game against the USSR and from Muckler's more defensive approach. Edmonton's goal scoring total suffered due to the team's new-found commitment to defence—dropping from 426 to 372 goals scored—but that output still led the league, the sixth straight year Edmonton sniped the most goals in the NHL. As a result, Edmonton owned the league's best record for a fourth time in five years. And despite Moog's workload advantage, Grant again was a Vezina finalist (eventually placing third behind Ron Hextall of the Flyers and the Whalers' Mike Liut).

Once the playoffs rolled around Grant received the nod to start against Los Angeles in round one. When he and his mates stumbled in a surprising 5–2 loss in Game 1 to the mediocre Kings, Moog took the reins for a couple of games. Andy enjoyed record goal support once Edmonton re-took control of the series in Game 2 with a 13–3 laugher that smashed a few NHL playoff marks in the process. But despite picking up another win in Game 3, Moog didn't sparkle in the 6–5 nail-biter. That earned Grant a chance to redeem himself. He would not relinquish control of the Edmonton net in a playoff game until an injury sidelined him in 1990. His Game 4 kicked off a remarkable string of 44 consecutive starts for Oiler playoff games, no doubt playing into Moog's departure the following year. Grant performed admirably enough in 6–3 and 5–4 wins to close out a surprisingly tough five-game series over L.A. From there he took his game to another level in a sweep of the Jets in the Smythe final, allowing just nine goals in the process. Next, he limited Steve Yzerman and the Red Wings to 10 goals in a five-game Campbell Conference final victory that sent Edmonton back to the Stanley Cup final against a familiar opponent.

Reclaiming their role as Stanley Cup champions would mean facing a challenge from Mike Keenan's Philadelphia Flyers and their pugnacious goalie Ron Hextall, a contender for Grant's title as the best goalie in the league. Philadelphia had knocked off Mats Naslund and Montreal in six games in an emotional Eastern final. Unfortunately for the Flyers, they had lost several stars to injury during their run, including offensive sparkplug Tim Kerr. Still, the favoured Oilers would have all they could handle fending off the injury-ravaged Flyers in the first final to go seven games since 1971. Grant allowed just 18 goals all series and was perhaps at the peak of his "money goalie" years. However, his rival Hextall took home the Conn Smythe Trophy as a result of his own courageous performance in the face of the Oilers' offensive fusillade. Part of the reason for the media's admiration for Hextall was his aggressive attitude toward Oilers forwards in his crease, contrasting with Grant's more stoic body language in the Edmonton net. Some observers thought that Hextall was passionate while Grant was simply steady. It was a great underestimation of the Fuhr Factor, and his performance in Game 7 would demonstrate his own worthiness for the Conn Smythe.

A young Grant Fuhr with his grandmother and cousins.
[credit: courtesy of the author]

Grant was named the 1979-80 WHL Rookie of the Year with the Victoria Cougars: it was no fluke, as the next season he was named WHL Goalie of the Year. [credit: Victoria *Times Colonist*]

Edmonton selected Fuhr (pictured here with Wayne Gretzky) with the 8th pick of the 1981 entry draft after Oilers head scout Barry Fraser told general manager Glen Sather that Grant was going to end up in the Hall of Fame. [credit: Miles Nadal/ Hockey Hall of Fame]

Grant Fuhr makes a save during the 1985 Stanley Cup Finals against Philadelphia, en route to the Oilers' second championship (and first of two against the Flyers). [credit: Paul Bereswill/Hockey Hall of Fame]

Fuhr was a member of two Canada Cup teams in 1984 and 1987, the latter a signature performance for Grant as he backstopped Team Canada to victory in a tournament many consider to have featured the finest hockey ever played. [credit: Paul Bereswill/Hockey Hall of Fame]

Grant Fuhr makes a save during Game 4 of the 1988 Stanley Cup Finals against Boston (which was actually game 5, as a power failure at Boston Garden caused the previous game to be suspended and replayed). Edmonton swept Boston for their third Stanley Cup, and Grant became the first NHL goaltender to win 16 games in a single playoff year. [credit: Paul Bereswill/Hockey Hall of Fame]

Along with the Canada Cup that preceded the season and the Stanley Cup that ended it, Grant was also awarded the 1987-88 Vezina Trophy as the NHL's best goaltender, voted on by the league's general managers. [credit: Doug MacLellan/Hockey Hall of Fame]

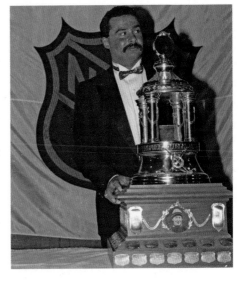

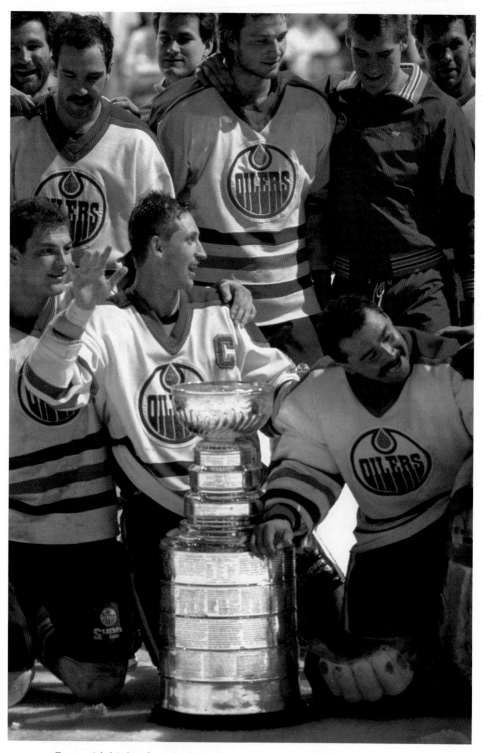

Grant with his hand on the Stanley Cup, the most coveted trophy in professional sports. The 1988 Stanley Cup was the Oilers' last with Wayne Gretzky. [credit: Paul Bereswill/Hockey Hall of Fame]

Prior to the 1991 season, Grant was traded to the Toronto Maple Leafs, whose legendary goalies Johnny Bower and Terry Sawchuk had been role models for Fuhr. [credit: Doug MacLellan/Hockey Hall of Fame]

In 1993, former Oilers head coach-turned-Buffalo general manager John Muckler traded for Fuhr. As a member of the Sabres, Grant would share the net with another future hall of famer, Dominik Hasek. [credit: Chris Relke/Hockey Hall of Fame]

Fuhr was briefly reunited with Wayne Gretzky in 1995 as a member of the Los Angeles Kings—a team Grant had known well since "The Miracle on Manchester." But Grant's Oilers had the overall edge against the Kings in the playoffs. [credit: Doug MacLellan/Hockey Hall of Fame]

Grant and Gretzky reunited a second time in St. Louis, where Fuhr signed as a free agent in the 1995 off-season. This photo was taken later at Wayne Gretzky's fantasy camp, and was the last time Grant ever played. [credit: courtesy of the author]

Fuhr ended his playing career in an unlikely place: Calgary, home of his longtime rivals, the Flames. There he was a mentor and inspiration to Fred Brathwaite and Jarome Iginla. [credit: Ronald C. Modra/ Sports Imagery/Getty Images]

5 rings for 5 Stanley Cup Championships: in 1984, 1985, 1987, 1988 and 1990. [credit: Gerry Thomas]

Grant with his son RJ and daughter Kendyl.

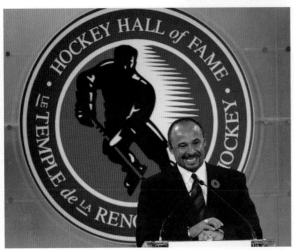

Grant Fuhr was inducted into the Hockey Hall of Fame in 2003, his first year of eligibility. [credit: Dave Sandford/Hockey Hall of Fame]

Grant Fuhr with his family on induction weekend. [credit: Dave Sandford/Hockey Hall of Fame]

For Grant, golf wasn't just a distraction for the off-season—it was a passion just like hockey. He continues to play scratch golf in tournaments like this one in Lake Tahoe. [credit: courtesy of the author]

Grant Fuhr with his old teammate Marty McSorley, with whom he played in Edmonton and Los Angeles. [credit: courtesy of the author]

Grant Fuhr with his daughter Kendyl, Matt Pendergast and Mark Messier. [credit: courtesy of the author]

The deciding game in Edmonton served as a perfect example of Grant's ability to shut the door when it mattered. "The Flyers received a two-man advantage just a minute into the game," McSorley recalled. "They scored once, but Grant kept the lead from growing after that. I think that might be his best moment I've ever seen." Messier and Kurri eventually gave the Oilers a 2–1 advantage they carried into the third period. With Edmonton nursing a slim lead against a desperate Flyers squad, Fuhr kept Philadelphia at bay for the final 23 minutes-plus in the decisive game. With Rick Tocchet, Scott Mellanby and Mark Howe pressing the Flyers attack, there were no openings for a tying goal with Grant in net, and Glenn Anderson added an insurance goal to end the game late in the third. The Oilers were champions again after a one-year hiatus, skating around the ice in Edmonton to the adulation of their fans. Grant was now the unquestioned No. 1 man in their net—and perhaps in the league.

Wayne Gretzky summed up his teammate for *Sports Illustrated*. "You have to understand that I mean no harm to the men who played in the '40s and '50s, but they played without masks. There is no way you could play without a mask today, against us, in this faster league. I've never seen reflexes like Grant's. I think he's the best goaltender in the history of the NHL. In two or three years, Ron Hextall may change that. But for now . . ."

Little did anyone know that Grant's performance in the 1987 Stanley Cup finals would not even be his greatest accomplishment of that year. A rematch with the Soviets lay ahead in the fall—a stirring showdown that might define his career.

For Canadian hockey fans of the Boomer generation there is only one possible defining game in their hockey pantheon: Canada's incredible 6–5 victory in Game 8 of the 1972 Summit Series. For younger fans, it might be Sidney Crosby's gold-medal overtime winner as Canada defeated the USA in the 2010 Vancouver Olympics. But for sheer skill and wizardry, there is nothing that compares to Game 2 of the three-game final series between Canada and the USSR at the 1987 Canada Cup. The series would be the only time in their pro careers that the two Canadian geniuses of offensive hockey, Mario Lemieux and Wayne Gretzky, played on the same team and (with brilliant results) on the same line for a brief while. It was the final time to see the legendary Soviet squad intact before political changes allowed their players to seek big money in the NHL. With Gretzky, Lemieux, Dale Hawerchuk and Ray Bourque leading Canada against the legendary Soviet attack of Igor Larionov, Sergei Makarov, Vladimir Krutov and Slava Fetisov, the three-game final series may have been the greatest orgy of scoring talent ever assembled.

Grant:

The Soviets were loaded that year. Every line could score. Krutov, Larionov, Makarov, Bykov, Fetisov, Kasatonov. Later I got to play with Alex Mogilny in Buffalo, and became good friends with Alex. He was a fourth-line guy at that time. Alex, Pavel Bure, Sergei Fedorov: not too shabby for the fourth line, right?

After the Oilers' third Stanley Cup championship in four years, Grant became the consensus favourite to start in the 1987 Canada Cup when training camps got underway in August. Canada's head coach Mike Keenan had seen first-hand only months earlier what Fuhr was capable of, and Iron Mike was predicted to tab Grant as the starter over his own Conn Smythe winner, Hextall. Keenan recognized the intangibles Grant brought to the biggest games.

"Grant was one on the most focused athletes I ever coached," Keenan reflected years later. "He was able to mentally prepare himself for every game by almost putting himself in a mental trance. Also, Grant's ability to quickly move mentally beyond any goal scored on him gave him a winning edge."

Grant, as was his custom, did not spend much time brooding over the decision of who would wear the maple leaf that fall.

Grant:

Never thought about it. Never worried about it. When I got the phone call telling me I was on the team, I was a little surprised. We'd finished in May. Then all of a sudden in August you're right back in training camp again. So it was a short summer. Right back at it. But it was fun because the same group of guys from Edmonton was there. You've got Glenn there, Mark's there, Wayne and Coff. So I guess it was a good time.

Keeping busy at the rink and away from other distractions was also a balm for Grant. And having the core of the Oilers team around also helped keep distractions at bay.

Grant:

We'd just come back from winning a Cup in 1987. You win a Cup and all of a sudden it's August, and it's serious hockey. Playing for your country—you don't take that lightly. You maybe didn't have the same urgency that you would have had if it was back in May or June for the final rounds of the playoffs. But you also had the same urgency to win. It's the same but different, if that makes sense.

As usual, Grant's summer training regimen had consisted of golf, more golf, and, if that didn't work, even more golf. When asked why he played 36 holes of golf between games that summer,

Grant drily noted, "Because it got too dark to play 54." But that pastoral approach to conditioning had yet to meet Mike Keenan. As Grant would discover later in St. Louis, Keenan had a penchant for fitness. Something was going to give when a well-rested Grant arrived at Team Canada's camp in late August 1987.

Grant:

Obviously, he already thought I was maybe not in the shape he thought I should be in. But I was also in the shape where I knew I could still play. So I got to pedal the bike a couple extra times with Wendel Clark. We had a good time laughing, because at certain points you'd say, "Okay, enough's enough, it's August." And Wendel, he'd just keep pedalling. I think he rode the extra minutes for me.

At that time Mike didn't push my buttons much—we had to wait until we were in St. Louis for that. Back then he would just make me ride the bike and let me play. Which was fine by me. There were a lot more choices and a lot of different angles that they were working on other than the goalies. So I got lucky at that time.

Keenan made a now-famous speech to the Canadian team in the '87 camp in which he asked the assembled players how many minutes were in a hockey game. "Sixty," came back the answer. "Wrong," said Keenan. "There are 360. Grant's going to get 60, Gretzk will get 25, Mess will get 23 . . ." Players soon saw that, while they were stars on their own teams, they were going to be lucky to get ice time with the stacked lineup representing Canada. Grant saw established players like Steve Yzerman, Al MacInnis, Scott Stevens and a future Keenan stalwart in Chicago, Denis Savard, cut from the team. Patrick Roy was one of the notable goalies left off. Keenan made his point about team concept in one pithy lesson.

Grant:

There were a lot of good hockey players that Mike had to let go. He could have made two really good hockey teams that could have won, just with the guys we had at camp. There were a lot of guys in your fourth line that are first-liners on any other team. It makes it interesting.

By the time the '87 Canada Cup rolled around, we'd played the Rendez-vous series earlier in '87. It was another chance to see some European hockey and get a chance to get a feel for it. The first time I experienced playing hockey against European teams, I learned their strategy is not to shoot from everywhere but to take a good shot. Something you have to learn again in a very short time. Different speed, different shot selection, that sort of thing. But it took some time to build back up again, and Russian teams were very good.

Thanks to the 1987 Rendez-vous games in February and the Calgary Olympic Games the following year, interest in international hockey from Canadian fans was at a fever pitch. After a lull since the NHL's first burst of international play in the '70s, there was once again genuine interest in how a Canadian team might fare against the world's best. Grant and the players on the team were about to undergo scrutiny that no Canadian team had experienced before.

Barely three months removed from winning the Stanley Cup, Grant found himself taken from his customary sleepy summer and thrust into the national pressure as the starter for Team Canada. Having won the job over Kelly Hrudey (who'd turn the tables later in Los Angeles with the Kings) and Ron Hextall, it was also his first chance to carry Canada in the finals of the Canada Cup, after injuring his shoulder in the 1984 tournament's round robin (where Rejean Lemelin took the starter's job in Fuhr's absence).

Grant:

In 1984 it wasn't too bad for the Canada Cup. It was still a fairly new event, then. The rivalry hadn't really got that nasty yet. So you didn't really have to worry about it. In '87, that changed. There was enough of it on the news that you knew it was a going to be a big deal, you knew enough from being in the dressing room it was a big deal.

If you went out in public you had to listen to it. But we weren't out in public the whole time. Everything was pretty sheltered. We all hung out as a group. We knew what was at stake for the country, but at the same time, you reminded yourself that it was still a hockey game. You'd played lots of games before, and in tough situations. You tried to look at it that way. I can tell you it would be a lot harder to play on Team Canada today with Twitter and Facebook and the 24-hour sports channels going at it all the time about who should make the team and who should be left off.

The Canadian lineup assembled by Hockey Canada was filled with players from the two teams featured in the most recent Cup final series, with Flyers and Oilers filling the roster. Besides Grant, Gretzky, Anderson and Coffey for Canada, the Flyers' Rick Tocchet, Brian Propp, Doug Crossman and Ron Hextall made the lineup for Keenan, their regular-season coach. One of the assistant coaches chosen for the squad was John Muckler, Keenan's acknowledgement for the role Muckler played in Edmonton's 1987 return to Cup glory. (Jean Perron and Tom Watt filled out the staff—this was clearly still before the days of goalie coaches.) Canada was favoured to win on the basis of its 1984 Canada Cup victory and the fact that so many of those stars were back for this tournament.

As the series progressed, however, fans and media started to believe that perhaps the early enthusiasm for a Canadian romp was a bit misplaced. After all, the Soviets had split the two games of the Rendez-vous in February—hardly a walkover. Despite a

3–0–2 record in round-robin action during the tournament, Canada hadn't exactly destroyed the competition once play began. Many of the wins were one-goal affairs that hung on a save one way or the other. A desperate comeback from down 3–1 against the Soviets in the round-robin portion salvaged a 3–3 tie in Canada's fifth contest at Hamilton's Copps Coliseum—the first meeting between the squads (Gretzky's goal with just 2:30 left had gained the tie). Grant stopped 33 of 36 Soviet shots he faced in a "spectacular" display, according to Tom McMillan of the *Pittsburgh Post-Gazette*. His performance was all the more impressive as Grant was learning on the fly about Soviets like future NHLer Valeri Kamensky.

Grant:

He was fast, fast and extremely good. At that time, too, we were still learning the Russian players. They weren't regulars in the NHL yet. You had basically a one-week window to try and figure out what everybody's strengths were. We thought about their star guys—that's all anybody talked about. Nobody talked about the back end of their teams. They're buzzing around me and I was like, "Who are these guys? They're not in my notes." You learned by trial and error.

The stirring comeback performance against the USSR earned the Canadians a semi-final rematch with a then-unknown goalie, Dominik Hasek of Czechoslovakia, who had registered a surprising 4–4 tie against Canada to open the tournament on August 28. Missing defected stars such as the Stasny brothers (who were banned by Czech officials for signing with the Quebec Nordiques), the Czechs were given little shot at beating Canada, with only 10,262 bothering to attend the game at the Montreal Forum. The ones who did show up, however, witnessed a dandy. After trailing

2–0 and being stymied by the acrobatic Hasek early in the semi-final, Canada eventually solved the Czech goaltender, prevailing 5–3 in the end. Grant faced 24 shots while Hasek had to deal with 37 from Team Canada. (Hasek would go on to become a teammate of Grant's with Buffalo a few years later.) Meanwhile, the USSR had beaten Sweden handily in the other semi-final. That set up a showdown with Canada in the best-of-three final.

In the first game, also held at the Forum, Grant was helpless to stop the early Soviet onslaught, and Canada fell behind 4–1 in the second period. Flashing their dazzling best, the Soviets scored a power-play goal and a short-handed marker from Sergei Makarov, a member of the KLM line with Igor Larionov and Vladimir Krutov. But a furious rally from Canada put the hosts ahead on a Wayne Gretzky goal with under three minutes left in regulation. It was short-lived; 32 seconds later, while the Forum PA announcer was still giving details of the Canadian goal, the USSR got a tying score on a nice re-direction by Andrei Khomutov on the doorstep of Grant's crease. In overtime, Alexander Semak (a future 37-goal scorer in the NHL with New Jersey) snapped a high blast off the crossbar from in close past a flailing Fuhr—and the Soviets had grabbed Game 1 by a count of 6–5. It was a humbling defeat for the favoured Canadians.

Grant:

Getting down 1–0 put a little bit of heat on us. We felt we probably should have won Game 1 after coming back from down three goals, but at the same time we gave them too many chances, and they could score. We learned from that.

The back-and-forth, high-scoring nature of Game 1 set the table for what was to come in Game 2 at Copps Coliseum. With Canada facing elimination, Game 2 produced arguably the most exciting, entertaining international hockey ever witnessed in a single game. Even with tremendous defenders such as Canada's Ray Bourque and Paul Coffey—or the USSR's Slava Fetisov and Alexei Kasatonov—there were chances galore and plenty of goals. Despite numerous key saves, including a stacked-pads beauty by Grant on Makarov just 30 seconds into the game, the score went into double digits. After the quick 4–1 start by the Soviets in Game 1, it was Canada that jumped into command early in Game 2. Quebec Nordiques defenceman Normand Rochefort, a surprise selection for Team Canada, completed a fine passing play to score and give Canada the early lead. Sparked by key saves from Grant on the penalty kill, Team Canada built a 3–1 margin in the first period with goals from Doug Gilmour and Coffey. But the Soviets fought back to tie the game in the second with goals from Fetisov on the power play and a short-handed marker from Krutov.

Doggedly, Canada built another lead in the second period, with Lemieux bulging the twine behind Evgeny Belosheikin to make it 4–3. Once more the Soviets responded, with Vyacheslav Bykov tying it at 4–4 just 4:45 later. In the third, Lemieux (playing at the top of his powers) struck to make it 5–4 on assists from Gretzky and Coffey. That lead didn't last either. After a concerted push by the Soviets to get the equalizer, a young Valeri Kamensky tied it at 5–5 with a brilliant individual effort. The future Quebec/ Colorado star forward wove through the Canadian defence at 18:56 of the third period, beating a poke-check from Grant to score high glove side, leaving the game headed to overtime again as the exhausted 17,026 fans in Copps Coliseum tried to catch their breath.

The classic match went through a heart-pounding 20-minute extra session with the ice tilted the way of the Soviets. Grant was called on to make 12 saves in a period dominated by the USSR. On one chance, Kasatonov and Larionov set up Krutov for a tip that Grant stymied by jamming shut the five hole. He then flashed his trademark catching hand, snaring the rebound from Krutov as well. As the horn sounded to end the first overtime, it seemed inevitable that Canada and Grant would succumb to the assault by the Soviet forwards in the summery warmth of the early September night in Hamilton. But Canada somehow found new legs. Halfway through the second OT, Mario Lemieux was left alone at the side of the net for the winner, assisted by—who else?—Wayne Gretzky. After 90 minutes and eight seconds of furious hockey, the series was tied at one game apiece. Canada still had life.

Despite another five goals allowed in Game 2, Grant was his usual unflappable self when reporters inquired about the pressure of a decisive Game 3.

Grant:
You'd like to think you could be perfect every day, but I was also taught that, for as much as you think you're going to be perfect, at some point the breaks go against you. Whether you like it or not, get over it and keep playing. If you gave up a goal, at some point you made a mistake. It doesn't matter how you look at it, at some point you had to have made a mistake for it to get by you. So I always believed the goal was more my mistake than anybody else doing something right. But I wasn't going to worry about it.

What would become the more famous finale of Game 3 was now set. Today, it's remembered for the three-way passing play on the winner scored by Lemieux with an assist from Gretzky. But it wouldn't have happened at all had Grant not stymied a great chance for the Soviets just moments before. As it was, Grant had

the best seat in the house to watch the play move up the ice with
Gretzky, Lemieux and Hawerchuk on the attack.

Grant:

I had the best view of the goal. I got to watch it go up the ice and develop.
After a little mad scrambling all around our end after the faceoff, we
broke up out on the rush. Gretzky has the puck, you've got Mario, you
had [Mike] Gartner up there. Hawerchuk was there. Gretz could have
passed it to Larry Murphy, too. They were wide open on the other side.
Any time Gretzky and Mario have control of it you're in pretty good hands.
Something good is going to happen. Once they scored the goal, we knew
that there were still two and a half, three minutes left. We'd seen how fast
they could score. But our guys were pretty good with that lead. It was one
we weren't going to let go of.

There was another factor in the series that was less heralded but
just as key, believes Grant. That was a momentum-shifting hit by
his Edmonton teammate Mark Messier.

Grant:

When he ran over Kasatonov that was vintage Messier. They were really
getting the momentum a little bit at that point. Mess pretty much stuck an
elbow on his chin and it changed the whole tide of the way things went.
He did that in a lot of different series. He did it against the Islanders; he
did it against Calgary a lot. He did it against Winnipeg. At any given time,
he could turn a game around just by knocking over somebody. But he
also had a finesse where he could score 40 goals. There's not a lot of
guys that have that package.

While the 6–5 win for Canada in Game 3 was a thriller, and
Grant played almost as well despite allowing five goals again,

Game 2 is widely considered today as the gem. Gretzky has referred to his five-assist performance in the second contest as the best game he ever played. While Lemieux never acknowledged as such, Game 2 may just have been Mario's best as well.

After the contest, reflecting on his team's effort, Wayne recognized Fuhr's important role, saying, "Grant has won so many games for us in goal that we have to take some of the burden off him." Overall, Grant posted respectable but not outstanding numbers in the Canada Cup, with a 3.34 GAA and .893 save percentage. But he played all nine tournament games after winning the job over Hextall and Hrudey, and, as ever, it was the timing of the saves he did make—the confidence he instilled that he would not give up the backbreaker—that buoyed Canada in its struggle to win the tournament. The media covering the games recognized this, and Grant was voted to the tournament's all-star team. Keenan, too, singled out Grant for his clutch play despite the five goals allowed. "Grant proved in 1987 to be the best goaltender in the world by winning both the Stanley Cup and Canada Cup. He was a true champion and one of the best goaltenders to ever play the game of hockey!"

The '87 showing was one of only three times Grant represented Canada internationally. As it turned out, Grant was the last Canadian to backstop a conquest of the Soviets at their peak as an international power, before glasnost and the dissolution of the USSR left Eastern European hockey in shambles through the mid-90s. It was a fitting cap to a 30-year rivalry that had come to define international hockey greatness, and the win could be seen as Grant's greatest contribution to the game in his country.

For Grant, the overtime heroics of Game 2 against the Soviets and the series itself crowned probably the greatest season of hockey ever experienced by a goalie: a Stanley Cup in the spring of 1987;

starts in Rendez-vous and the 1987 all-star game; Vezina Trophy winner: and hero of the hockey nation for his performances at Copps Coliseum in Hamilton. "I don't think we'll ever see another season like that from a goalie again," says Keenan. "He was everything you could ask for back there."

Talk about redemption.

GAME 6

During the first years of Grant's career it would have been a stretch to call him an ironman capable of carrying the full workload of a Stanley Cup winner. Coming off his triumph in the 1987 Canada Cup, Grant was at the top of his craft (even if he wasn't being paid like it by the Oilers ownership), but he'd been evenly dividing the workload in the Edmonton net with Andy Moog since his rookie year of 1981–82. That was about to change. While rumours continued to circulate in Edmonton's close hockey community about Grant's private life, there was no doubting that the Oilers' local product was only getting better on the ice. Now that his longtime partner Moog was with the Canadian Olympic team, holding out for a trade out of Edmonton, Grant's starts ballooned. In his first year as the acknowledged No. 1, he zoomed to 75 regular-season and 19 playoff starts in 1987–88. Not only did he step up his workload, he won his only Vezina Trophy as the NHL's top goaltender that year, and finished second in voting for the Hart Memorial Trophy as league MVP, behind Mario Lemieux and ahead of teammate Wayne Gretzky.

The jump in starts alarmed some who thought it would burn out the five-foot-nine-inch goalie. Could he physically sustain the pace? What about his mental makeup under the increased duty? During the season, Sather grew bored with people asking if Grant was being overworked. "I'm not amazed at all Grant can play that many games," Sather told the *Boston Globe*. "I am amazed that people ask the same questions about it. Did you see Larry Bird the other night? He plays all the time. Or how about Ray Bourque? There's a guy I'm amazed with. He plays 40 minutes a game on defense. Grant Fuhr stands in front of the net for 60 minutes. Glenn Hall and Jacques Plante did the same thing for their entire careers and they didn't wear masks. Grant is a young guy. Why should he be tired mentally?"

Fuhr's play certainly didn't reflect any fatigue. Former roommate Ron Low summed up his protegé for *SI*: "Grant reads the game as well as any goalie that has ever played. His goals-against average will never be the best. He'll give up the occasional soft goal. But in the big moment, for the big save, he's 95 percent unbeatable. Under pressure, there is none finer. He proved in the Canada Cup that he is the finest goaltender in the world."

Grant then proved his value to the Oilers in more than durability. His critics said he had been the lucky recipient of being on a team with the greatest offence ever. But with Gretzky shelved for 16 games and producing a "pedestrian" 149-point total in 1987–88, Grant's reliability in goal was needed more than ever. He provided his team with some of his most stellar numbers, posting a career-high 40 wins, a 3.43 GAA (the lowest since his rookie year) and four shutouts—by far the most he'd had in a single season. For the natural athlete who once relied upon his reflexes and unpredictability, there was suddenly some method to his seeming madness between the posts.

Grant:

Each year you're trying to add something. I think if you get stale and
try and work with only one thing you have, they figure you out at some
point. You've got to give them different looks, and try and learn something
yourself, to try and get better every year. As I got older, obviously I wasn't
getting any quicker, so now you have to get a little bit smarter: able to
play angles a little bit better, read the game a little bit better, which will
make you look just as quick as you ever were—but it's more that you
have a sense of what's going on. It's all trying to look the same while doing
different things.

In the 1988 playoffs, the Oilers showed that, like their goalie,
they'd been learning from the past few seasons of defensive
preaching by co-coach John Muckler. Their offence continued to
churn out goals by the bushel, but their back end was now as
tight as the best defensive squads in the NHL. Which was a good
thing for any team playing in the shooting gallery known as the
Smythe Division.

Grant:

Three of, probably, the top six teams in the league were just in our division.
It wasn't even in our conference; it was just our division. Any time you
played Winnipeg, you played Calgary—Vancouver was okay at that time—
the hardest part was to get out of your own division. Every year it was us
and Calgary right out of the gate. One of us would get either L.A. or
Vancouver: somebody got an easy one, and somebody got the battle of
Winnipeg every year. With Dale [Hawerchuk] they were always a challenge.

In the first round of the 1988 playoffs, it was the Oilers who had
their hands full with Winnipeg, finally prevailing four games to
one over the pesky Jets. That brought them another dance with the

hated Calgary Flames in Round 2. Over the course of the decade, Calgary GM Cliff Fletcher had assembled a very talented squad at the Saddledome with veterans such as Lanny McDonald and Hakan Loob meshing with the products of the Flames' deep farm system, Al MacInnis and Theo Fleury. Sharp trades had brought Doug Gilmour and John Tonelli to the Flames as well. With Calgary's 105 regular-season points good enough for the Presidents' Trophy, there were whispers that Edmonton might finally have met its match. Calgary had scored more goals (398 to the Oilers' 363) and had their own proven playoff goalie in Mike Vernon to match Grant.

Someone forgot to tell the Oilers—still keenly feeling the sting of the 1986 Steve Smith goal—that they were through. Led by Grant, who allowed just 11 goals in the four games, they buried the first-place Flames. The beat-down started with a sweep of the first two games on the road at the Saddledome. The back-breaker came after the Flames had blown a two-goal lead in Game 2. A highlight-reel short-handed goal in overtime by Gretzky then ended it as he streaked down the left wing, blasting a laser to the far side over Vernon's catching glove. Game 3 in Edmonton brought a scare as Joel Otto of the Flames ripped a drive off Grant's collarbone early in the second period. The entire Northlands crowd hushed as Grant writhed in pain on the ice: Who could withstand such a shot without being badly hurt? Then, like Rod Tidwell in *Jerry Maguire*, Grant bounced back up on his skates, seemingly as good as new. Pain would not stop No. 31; the Flames were going to have to beat him the conventional way. A five-minute major penalty to Oilers defenceman Marty McSorley was overcome without incident and Calgary's Game 3 hopes died right there. With revenge for 1986 at hand, Edmonton wasted no time. Game 4 showed the mighty Oilers offence in peak form as they outscored

Calgary 6–4. Any Battle of Alberta talk seemed settled as the Flames crawled home, swept out by their acrobatic nemesis from Edmonton.

After drubbing the Detroit Red Wings four games to one in the Conference finals, the Oilers faced their old teammate Moog and the Boston Bruins in a bid for a fourth Stanley Cup in five years. This was the legacy year for Sather's team, the chance to leap from excellent to great. The final was no contest as the Oilers surrendered just nine goals in the four completed games (one game in Boston was abandoned due to a power failure). The Oilers' 16–2 record that post-season is still the best winning percentage in the four-round era since 1979–80, and Grant backstopped every minute along the way. At this point he was finally getting help from his defence as the Oilers regularly held opponents to under 25 shots during this run—one in which every facet of the team truly shone, and there seemed to be no evident trace of weakness.

"Nothing at all bothers him," said Grant's Victoria teammate Geoff Courtnall, now in Edmonton. "He is so relaxed, yet he is one of the quickest goalies in the league. Some guys get beat on a shot and they let down, get caught on a couple more quick ones. With Grant it's the exact opposite. He responds to the challenge and plays even better."

With a fourth Stanley Cup in the bag, the Oilers and their fans prepared for the Hollywood-style wedding of Gretzky and actress Janet Jones in Edmonton on July 16, 1988. National television coverage and a breathless Hollywood paparazzi brought every last sequin on Janet's $40,000 ensemble to the attention of a waiting world. While Edmonton firemen formed an honour guard on the steps of St. Joseph's Basilica, the Edmonton Symphony played the transitional music. Celebrities in the church ranged from actor Alan Thicke to Mr. Hockey himself, Gordie Howe. Grant had front row seats for the hockey "wedding of the century."

Grant:

Oh yeah, third or fourth row, at the front. It was something. Everybody turned out, dressed to the nines. One of the few times I ever wore a suit in those days, especially in the summer. Gretz never seemed to get bothered by the attention. But we'd been watching Wayne for years, and by that point, nothing really surprised us. Well, I should say the *next* thing that happened to him that summer surprised us.

Grant was in his customary summer residence on a golf course on August 9, playing in Bob Cole's tournament in St. John's, Newfoundland, with teammate Marty McSorley (or a guy Grant thought was still his teammate) when the shocking rumours that Gretzky would no longer be an Oiler were confirmed. "I didn't know till I called my agent, Mike Barnett, after I'd heard that Gretz had been traded," recalls McSorley. "And I was saying 'You can't tear this team apart, you have to stop this.' Mike said, 'Sit down, I think you're in the trade.'"

Grant:

We were out playing in Bob Cole's golf tournament. People kept coming up to us, and we were hearing these stories about a trade. Marty thought everybody was kidding him that he'd been traded to Los Angeles with Gretz. I hadn't heard anything about it. Turns out they'd been talking all summer about it. So that was a little shocking. You knew there were some contract issues and Peter [Pocklington] was having troubles financially. I was having my contract troubles with Glen. But Gretz? No way.

As Garth and Wayne liked to say, "Way." The deal that shocked Canada was Wayne Gretzky, Marty McSorley, and Mike Krushelnyski to the Los Angeles Kings in exchange for Jimmy Carson, Martin Gelinas, the Kings first-round draft picks in 1989, 1991 and 1993, and $15 million. Almost as surprising to NHL players was the fat new contract Gretzky got after the trade. Kings owner Bruce McNall felt his new star need to be paid like a star and awarded No. 99 $3 million a year for five years. (Gretzky's agent, Mike Barnett, revealed later that the centre had actually requested a lower salary, concerned the Kings could not then afford the other players to produce a champion. McNall laughed him off.) The Gretzky contract was a tide that would soon raise all salary boats for NHL players. Told for decades by the NHL and their own union leader, Alan Eagleson, that there wasn't much money in the hockey business, they suddenly discovered that a pot of gold lay in Los Angeles and other major cities. As important as Gretzky was to the popularization of hockey in the Sun Belt, he was equally as important to his fellow players, such as Grant, who would eventually collect millions in salary over the rest of their careers.

That salary tide was bad news for Edmonton, however, where the same business travails that had forced owner Peter Pocklington to make the Gretzky trade now made raises little more than a dream for the remaining Oilers players. Just how tight the Edmonton salary pinch was in 1988 was demonstrated the summer before as Grant's new agent, Ritch Winter, got into a metaphorical shoving match with Sather over getting market value for his client. Winter was a new breed of agent, not beholden to the Alan Eagleson–imposed regime at the NHL Players' Association. In exchange for having a free hand to exploit international hockey, Eagleson was running a house union that allowed teams to suppress salaries for top players. In particular, Eagleson did not believe in salary disclosure among players—a practice that had catapulted salaries in other pro sports into the stratosphere. Winter felt the players' salaries were artificially held down by the lack of free agency in the business, and Fuhr's case (the best goalie in the NHL making $300,000 a year, far less than other NHL goalies, and with no leverage) was Exhibit A. Winter knew teams such as Detroit would pay more—a lot more—for the best goalie in the game. But Sather, paid to hold the line on a budget imposed by Pocklington, disagreed. Moreover, Sather held the hammer in deciding where Grant would play.

The acrimony from Grant's contract talks would linger until his departure from the Alberta capital. Meanwhile, the stunned Oilers tried to figure out life without their captain.

Grant:

At camp the guys rallied around each other and decided they wanted to win again to show it wasn't just a fluke. Everybody probably pushed a little harder that year. Especially when we knew we'd be facing Gretz during the season.

For Grant, the first season without No. 99 as a teammate would prove his most frustrating yet as a pro. Coming off personal triumph the season before, 1988–89 was a letdown. The year from hell began with Grant missing the start of the season due to a knee injury suffered in training camp. He would barely have time to prepare for the return of Gretzky to Northlands in a Kings uniform on October 19. The mid-week game would be broadcast nationally and attract a huge media swarm. Gretzky himself would receive a four-minute standing ovation from the Edmonton crowd. For Grant, facing his old friend would be a novelty—and a challenge.

If there was one person in the Edmonton Oilers dressing room who could truly appreciate what Wayne Gretzky did for a hockey team, it was Grant Fuhr. From the time of his arrival with the Oilers in 1981 until Gretzky's departure in 1988, Grant had had to face the greatest scoring machine in NHL history every day in practice and every training camp in scrimmages. Gretzky liked to score goals—and he didn't spare the feelings of his own goalie in the process.

Grant:

People say you're lucky not to have faced him in games all those years. But I used to go up against him in practice every day. He liked to score, and he didn't like to be embarrassed, even in practice. We had some good battles. We pushed each other to be that much better. I was okay with him being a hero and having the fans cheer him in Edmonton. I understood it had nothing to do with me. But I was not giving him a hat trick to please anyone.

The 8–6 Oilers win featured a vintage Gretzky performance, with chances galore. Grant repelled 31 of the 37 Kings shots thrown at him. An emotional Gretzky didn't score against Grant—but he did collect two assists, finishing -2 on the night. The perfect homecoming scenario was ruined for Gretzky not by Grant but by the Kings' goalie Glenn Healy, who stopped just 13 of the 21 shots sent his way.

After the game, Gretzky did his best to deflect any blame for his trade. "I'm still proud to be a Canadian," he told reporters. "I didn't desert my country. I moved because I was traded, and that's where my job is. But I'm Canadian to the core. I hope Canadians understand that."

For Grant, the showdown win might have been the high-water mark of the regular season. A cervical neck strain sidelined him in January and his .875 save percentage was his worst in seven years.

His 3.83 GAA was only slightly above his career average at the time, but it came in front of a more experienced, defensively stout team than the ones he'd played for a few years earlier.

As a team the Oilers had just 84 points in 1988–89, by far their worst winning percentage since 1980–81. In Gretzky's absence, Jari Kurri stepped up as the overall leading scorer, while Jimmy Carson (obtained in the Gretzky trade) topped the club with 49 goals. Bill Ranford—acquired in the Moog trade— would soon be pushing Grant for the starter's job after starting 29 games while Grant was hurt or resting. But it would still be No. 31 starting in the Edmonton net for the 1989 playoffs. And as fate would have it, the Oilers drew Gretzky and the Kings in the first round—which meant a few more emotional games in Edmonton for the two teams.

Grant:

He had played against me just about everyday in practice, so it was fun to want to play against him in games. It was fun just to see, more than anything, how it would go. You take it as a personal challenge. You'd seen everything in practice. You've just never seen it live in a game coming at you, where you actually worry about it. It makes it look a little different. Having done it now I can say it's just as impressive live as it is in practice. He made it look just as easy.

The series started off well enough for the Oilers. They seized a 3–1 series lead with only 11 goals surrendered by Grant—includ-ing his second career playoff shutout with a 4–0 win in Game 3. But then, out of nowhere, the vaunted Oilers magic in the clutch disappeared. (Or perhaps it just migrated to the Kings bench.) They'd always found a way to win before, but now that extra gear disappeared in the face of a Gretzky hungry for vindication—for the trade away from Edmonton and for Pocklington's criticism of the man who'd made the franchise. In part, the capitulation to the Kings was due to Grant losing his game while L.A. goalie Kelly Hrudey simultaneously regained his own mojo. Grant was victimized for several weak goals amongst the 13 that got by him as the Kings took three straight to clinch the series. Game 7 was particularly tough. After the Kings went ahead 5–3 in the third period off a controversial goalie-interference non-call, Fuhr snapped on the officiating crew. He threw his stick into the crowd, earning an unsportsmanlike conduct penalty. It was uncharacteristic behaviour for the fun-loving Fuhr of old, but it summed up his rocky first season without Gretzky.

An empty netter sealed the loss, and while the Oilers put on smiles for the handshakes with their old friend, there was a deep sense of disappointment and perhaps even a sense that they were at the end of an era. After having the hockey world by the tail in 1987–88, Grant was now suddenly eliminated early in April. As he sat in a sombre Edmonton dressing room, Grant finally knew how it felt to lose to the man they called the Great One. Seeing their old friend and former inspiration put a dagger in the season was yet another sign that the Oilers of old, the core of the team Grant had come to in 1981, was slowly being taken apart. The frustration of the series would boil over in his contract negotiations with Glen Sather that summer.

Grant:

You know once Gretz is gone things are starting to dismantle. When they traded Gretz in 1988 and you read the different articles about the money and such in Edmonton, then you kind of get a grasp of it. Coffey was moved out. Gretzky was gone. Andy was gone. Messier was having issues at that time, contract-wise. Part of that was me being young at the time and not knowing the economics of the game. You see other guys on other teams getting bigger contracts—and we're winning but making nothing like them. So you know at some point you're moving, too. Even though you don't want to, at some point you know it's going to happen.

With no playoff hockey on the agenda, Grant once again took up the offer to play for Team Canada, this time at the World Hockey Championships in Sweden. Getting away from Edmonton and the stinging headlines in the media seemed like a good strategy. Winning a silver medal for Canada was gratifying, but for a man accustomed to Stanley Cup and Canada Cup titles it was no replacement for another championship. And it was no bulwark against the troubles confronting Grant off the ice.

Personal and professional issues came to a head that summer as Grant and Winter continued to pressure the financially challenged Oilers into paying Grant his value as the NHL's best goalie. As a means of expanding Grant's income, Winter had come up with a novel plan to have Grant wear the Pepsi-Cola logo on his goal pads in 1989–90. It was a creative idea, but one that faced a huge roadblock. The NHL did not allow (and still does not allow) individual players to promote products on their uniforms. Winter felt that if the Oilers could not afford to pay Grant his market value, they should at least fight to have an exemption made that would allow Fuhr to make up the difference. Winter, who was launching an attempt to unseat Eagleson as the head of the NHLPA, also accused the Oilers of cheating their players by trading Wayne Gretzky so that none of them could earn their projected bonus money for the 1988–89 season. Needless to say, Sather categorically denied the accusation.

No wonder there were rumours that Grant might join Gretzky in Los Angeles that summer (in exchange for $5 million). Kings owner Bruce McNall did not dampen the speculation. "Peter Pocklington and I talk all the time," he told the *Boston Globe*. "If the opportunity was there, I'd have to consider it. If Peter Pocklington wants to make that deal, I'm all ears." Pocklington, who'd already been savaged over the Gretzky deal and was hard for cash, tried to stickhandle. "I have no interest in selling off anybody," Pocklington was quoted as saying. "Grant Fuhr isn't worth $5 million. . . . I never say never about anything, but Wayne Gretzky was once-in-a-lifetime." To which No. 99 added, "If Oilers owner Peter Pocklington decides to sell Grant Fuhr and Mark Messier, I should think the general manager would have to quit."

Though the trade rumours floated publicly, much of the personal conflict between Winter and Sather happened behind the scenes. So when Grant and Winter, seated on a golf cart, met the media on June 8, 1989, to announce the netminder's retirement at age 26, there was genuine shock from the fans and even some of the press. Looking decidedly uncomfortable, Grant said, "If you can't play this game and have fun and get the respect you deserve then there's not much reason for going on," he told the reporters huddled around the cart. "This has been a long time coming, a long time building up." Saying he'd been belittled from the beginning by the Oilers, Grant suggested he didn't have the respect of his teammates either, adding that he would rather sell cars at an Edmonton-area dealership than play under licensing restrictions (likely referring to a dealership in Wetaskiwin, Alberta, in which he had invested). Winter and Fuhr claimed that this was a battle for players' rights; naysayers, however, suggested that Winter had actually orchestrated the entire drama to force a renegotiation on Fuhr's long-term contract.

The news that the best goalie in the league was packing it in at 26 sent shock waves through the NHL. As power plays go, this was an enormous gamble by a player in the prime of his career—especially one who had a promising young backup waiting to take over. But the holdout strategy had worked for Grant's teammates Moog and Paul Coffey, who had both engineered deals out of Edmonton. Winter and Sather were already arguing over the contract for another of Winter's clients, Esa Tikkanen, and Winter was gambling that the retirement threat would force Sather to trade Grant to Detroit, where he would be able to boost his pay. In practice, however, Edmonton held all the cards under the owner-friendly collective bargaining agreement negotiated by Eagleson for the NHLPA. Sather could sit tight and wait until Fuhr and Winter blinked. To ratchet up the pressure, Sather announced he was cutting off talks with Winter, making the agent himself an issue in the negotiation.

On June 8, 1989, Fuhr presented signed retirement papers to Sather, which, if filed with the NHL, would force Furh to sit for the 1989–90 season. Convinced the retirement was nothing more than a negotiating ploy, Sather held onto the papers until training camp to see if Fuhr was serious about quitting. Sather growled at the implications of poor treatment from the team. "Grant Fuhr has been treated with kid gloves from Day 1," he told reporters. "If Grant wants to retire, the world isn't going to stop because he's not here. If Grant wants to quit, I'll sign Pete Peeters. He's a free agent without compensation." Ironically, just five days after Grant stirred up his hornet's nest with his retirement tactic, Sather stepped down as Oilers head coach, handing the reins full-time to Muckler, who'd been operating as a de facto head coach for awhile.

As media criticism of Winter mounted, and as Grant acknowledged he really didn't want to retire, the situation was finally resolved in a two-hour meeting between Fuhr and Sather on August 24, 1989. Following that meeting, Fuhr announced he was not going to retire and would report to Edmonton's training camp as scheduled.

Grant:

I don't know if I was searching for something or maybe just a little bit lost in space. Ritch [Winter] had some great ideas. I liked the advertising on the pads; I thought that was actually a really good idea. But the holdout wasn't going to get anything accomplished. You just get the fans on you, which is never good. Nothing ever gets accomplished out of it.

Yeah, I got a new deal, but it was the same deal I would have gotten anyhow. And now I'd pissed everybody off to get the same deal.

Grant willingly walked away from the Pepsi deal, but said he was surprised to find out that the NHL, rather than the Oilers, was responsible for his not being allowed to put the logo on his pads. Winter still argued that the NHL did not have the right to ban the Pepsi pads, but his client had already lost interest in the arrangement. Fuhr would drop Winter as his agent on September 27, saying he was uncomfortable with Winter's negotiating tactics and that Winter had not always acted in his best interest.

Grant:

Yeah, he did a lot that was good for me. But Ritch just had a different style than the one I have. I don't need to rock the boat and cause all sorts of grief and have people upset. I liked being in Edmonton; I was happy being in Edmonton. I didn't need to turn that into a disaster. Unfortunately, I think Ritch was trying to change the Players' Association at my expense. I happened to be in the middle of all that shrapnel. Bad choice on my part maybe. But so be it; it happened.

The summer's retirement drama was a foreshadowing of more serious issues to come in Grant's life. In September of '89, he and his wife, Corrine, split. On top of this came an emergency appendectomy, which caused Grant to miss the start of the season. When Grant finally did return, he was not sharp. While he started 15 of the next 21 games, Ranford was the hotter goalie. Worse, in a 3–3 tie with St. Louis on December 19, Grant aggravated a shoulder injury that had previously required surgery—with a recovery time estimated at over two months.

The Oilers were in a bind during Grant's rehabilitation period, uncertain that the impressive young Bill Ranford could carry a full load in the playoffs. Indirectly, the team suggested that it would be helpful if their star goalie could find his way back from rehab in time for the end of the season. So Grant returned early on March 3, 1990, against Philadelphia. Looking like the Fuhr of old, he out-duelled longtime rival Ron Hextall. Grant stopped 35 of 38 shots in a 5–3 win that sparked hope the old Grant Fuhr was back on the case. But just three games later, he reinjured the same shoulder. This time there was no doubt: surgery was necessary. He was done for the season. A disappointing 9–7–3 record, 3.89 GAA and mediocre .868 save percentage were the final insults on a year gone bad.

With Eldon "Pokey" Reddick—another African-Canadian goalie—occupying the backup role, Ranford took over the Oilers' No. 1 job. After a slow start that saw Edmonton down 3–1 in their opening series with Winnipeg, Ranford energized the Oilers. First he helped the Oilers overcome the 3–1 deficit, beating the Jets in seven games. Then came a revenge sweep of Gretzky's Kings to take the Smythe Division. As Ranford's momentum built, the Oilers next toppled the Chicago Blackhawks in six games to win the Campbell Conference.

Once again the Oilers found themselves back in a Stanley Cup Final, this time powered by Mark Messier and Bill Ranford—not Wayne Gretzky and Grant Fuhr. They were also helped by the addition of young forwards Adam Graves and Joe Murphy, obtained from Detroit for a disgruntled Jimmy Carson. Alongside Martin Gelinas, who'd come in the Gretzky deal, they formed a Kid Line that sparked the veteran core of the team.

Shining his brightest in the five-game Cup Finals against Boston, Ranford allowed only eight goals in a little under 18 periods of hockey. It was a performance befitting Grant Fuhr—but Ranford, the understudy, did Grant one better by taking home the Conn Smythe Trophy as playoff MVP to boot. Grant was a pleased teammate, winning a fifth Stanley Cup ring, but being in street clothes for what turned out to be his final Stanley Cup celebration took the shine off the joyous occasion. As he headed into the summer, Grant was no longer the unquestioned name on the goaltending marquee in Edmonton. He would have to win back his job or move somewhere he could play—and be paid—as a No. 1 goalie.

GAME 7

For Grant Fuhr, veteran of hundreds of NHL games in the regular season and playoffs, the pre-game anticipation for this one contest in the midst of a long NHL season was excruciating. As he rhythmically rocked back and forth in his goal crease at the Brendan Byrne Arena, "The Star Spangled Banner" seemed to never end. To hurry up the music, Grant scraped at the ice, preparing it for the game ahead—his first in almost a year. On the bench, his Edmonton teammates waited anxiously to see if the restless goalie in the crease was still their go-to guy. A Canadian national TV audience and the entire league waited, too. Would the most successful goalie of the decade still be able to play after being away for so long, and after tearing up his shoulder the previous year?

Grant:
It went by really slowly. You're waiting. You've got to get through the national anthems—that's the hardest part. It's the waiting, waiting, waiting. You go through the morning skate, then you try to get your afternoon nap. Now you've got to wait, wait, wait. Once the game starts, you're comfortable. Because it's the one place that you're always comfortable: on the ice.

You're not really sure about how it's going to go or what's going to happen, and you don't know if you've lost it because you haven't played an NHL game in months.

Once the game got going it felt like I'd never missed a beat. Until then, however, it'd felt like I was waiting forever.

For someone who'd been playing hockey since the age of four, going so long without stopping a puck was a jarring experience. Most athletes only face this kind of anxiety when coming back from injury. But Grant's anxiety stemmed from a different place. His lengthy hiatus was not due to his balky shoulders or a wonky knee. This time, the layoff came courtesy of a league suspension for substance abuse. Everyone in the arena and watching on TV knew about his five Stanley Cups, his Canada Cup, the All-Star berths and the legendary Oilers. But now a darker part of his past had been exposed to the public. His secret life had caught up to him.

Stories of wild times with the Edmonton Oilers were nothing new. An infamous 1986 *Sports Illustrated* article had dissected the Oilers' playoff demise against the Calgary Flames and levelled serious allegations about rampant drug use by five or six nameless Oilers. Predictably, the Oilers defended themselves from the accusations, blasting *SI* for having little proof and relying on unnamed sources. At the time, Sather commented, "This entire article has been taken out of context with no reasonable backup. . . . If someone on this club was convicted of using drugs, he wouldn't be here any longer." In the same 1986 article, Fuhr firmly denied any drug use.

These were the same denials he'd given Sather ever since the Oilers' GM and coach first heard rumours from the Edmonton community about Grant's lifestyle. Sather still had his suspicions, but he couldn't uncover proof or get Grant to confess. In public,

Sather defended Grant and his team, saying no athlete could possibly have a raging drug habit and perform at the level the Oilers did. During the 1987 documentary *The Boys on the Bus*, Sather can be seen saying he was "absolutely positive that there can't be a guy that plays professional hockey and has a serious drug problem. I think that guys have been exposed to drugs in this league, as in any walk of life. . . . In the NHL, there can't be one guy who could be hooked on any kind of drugs and play on a regular basis. You'd have to notice it—the trainers, the doctors, I mean everyone."

Still, the rumours and innuendoes would not go away. The uneasy standoff between the facts and denials continued through the glory years of the '80s as Grant tried to keep his private and public lives from intersecting.

But that ended when his now ex-wife Corrine decided to tell her story to the *Edmonton Journal* in the summer of 1990. It was a sensational tale of unpaid utility bills, of angry phone calls from suppliers—and of how the Oilers management had learned of his issues in the later years of the Oilers Cup runs. Before publication, the *Journal* asked Grant to respond to the piece. Faced with the inevitability of the exposé, and wanting to lighten the weight of the secret he carried, he unburdened himself. Grant explained that he had been using a "substance" since 1983 or 1984, and had used it on binges every three to four weeks. He also revealed that he had repeatedly lied to Edmonton general manager Glen Sather when questioned about possible drug use. Now the time had come to tell the truth.

Grant:

I probably could have sat there and said nothing, and there's probably no way they could have ever proven anything. Deny, deny, deny. And then it would have hung there forever. It was easier to get it out and move on. I didn't have a problem getting it out. I mean, it was part of my life—it had happened. I wasn't proud of it, but it was also done by then. So I thought, "Okay, yeah, I made that mistake. Maybe I should seek some help."

Life needed to be straightened out a little bit. There was no question about that, so I went down to a program called the Straight Program in St. Petersburg, Florida, which was for adolescents. And it wasn't so much the program that was an eye-opener for me as the kids in there with me. That was probably a bigger influence than anything. Hearing their stories, seeing them: I mean, they were having a hard time. And it was a drug culture that I'd never seen before: Florida has a way more serious problem than Edmonton. There was a lot more that I never knew existed, which was another big eye-opener. Made what we were doing seem kind of inconsequential at the time. But at the same time you also didn't want to be in that boat, because it didn't look like it was very much fun for them.

Coming after so many years of rumours, the acknowledgement of substance problems wasn't a complete surprise to people in the Edmonton community or the NHL at large. They were used to tales of Grant's unique behaviour. But the tales of a loveable flake couldn't remove the shock of hearing how one of the NHL's greatest stars had battled a substance problem while performing brilliantly at the top of the sport. "What surprises me the most is that he carried us," Wayne Gretzky recalled later. "To be able to play at the level he played at for all those years [while on drugs] is a surprise."

Later, *SI* would expand on the story. In March 1991 it was written that when Grant was the premier goalie in the game, he "could not say no to cocaine. He spoke in monosyllables and wore a what-me-worry facade that hid his insecurities. 'You could talk to him,' [said] teammate Ken Linseman, 'but you couldn't *really* talk to him.'"

The revelations provoked a media firestorm that rapidly engulfed Grant.

Grant:

I'd just come back from L.A., and they had a bunch of reporters sitting in the airport when we landed. So we're driving home and I got the phone call from Slats that we should probably have a meeting. It was suggested I go to another facility in Palm Springs called the Betty Ford Center. I'd gone to Florida before that, because you could sneak in and sneak out. I spent two weeks there, and got released after two weeks. But I agreed to come down to the Betty Ford for a 10-day assessment. That was my first time in Palm Springs. What's ironic is that I live five minutes from there now.

After 10 days I got told that I didn't need to be there any longer. The Oilers owners were having a golf tournament in Palm Springs at the same time. So I was released, and I joined the team for the tournament. Then I went back to Edmonton with the team.

Back in Edmonton, Grant didn't dodge the story, telling the *Edmonton Sun* that his time under the influence was "the darkest period of my life. A million apologies can't change what I've done. I have to live with that fact for the rest of my life. I think I can play this game again and be the best. I don't think I've lost any talent, but I have to go out and regain my self-esteem and confidence as a person."

While Grant might have thought that confessing would help him put his past behind him, the NHL had other ideas. The league reacted by scheduling a hearing on the matter, set for September 26, 1990. Grant was allowed to attend the Oilers' training camp in the weeks prior to the hearing, but he was banned from playing in pre-season games. At the time, the NHL under president John Ziegler had an ad-hoc, no-tolerance approach that insisted players who used illegal drugs would face automatic suspensions. The league, which had no official drug-penalty policy, had been tainted in the past by drug stories, with players such as Don Murdoch, Borje Salming and Bob Probert being slapped with lengthy suspensions. Still, there was a suspicion that the use of recreational and performance-enhancing drugs was growing within the league. Grant Fuhr was going to be a juicy fastball for NHL president John Ziegler to hit out of the park when the two met.

Grant:

I got the pleasure of meeting Mr. Ziegler face to face. Sat down with him. The vice-president of the league at that time, Brian O'Neill, he was there, and a league attorney. Glen was there. It was actually all very cordial. They asked me for a couple of thoughts and opinions. Then Ziegler opened the conversation by saying he was a Diet Coke addict—that was his opening line, his idea of a joke. So I knew it was not going to be good. They said that they would take everything under advisement and think about it. Which, to this day, I still think was pre-planned before we ever went. I actually think it was a waste of time going. Needless to say, we weren't very happy with it, but greater minds than mine decide those things.

The biggest misconception about that period of time is that the substance problem was still ongoing—but by the time it finally hit the paper it had been two years over and long stopped, over and done. So they were dredging up stuff that had happened two and three years before. I might have needed an intervention back then, but Mr. Ziegler was a little late. Things had already started to turn around at that point. So do we really need this now? No. But, at the same time, it's all finally out. It's not something I ever to have to worry about again.

Grant and the Oilers hoped that owning up to his past and having been clean for a year might mitigate the sentence, but they were bitterly disappointed. On September 27, 1990, the NHL announced that Fuhr would be suspended one year for what John Ziegler termed conduct "dishonorable and against the welfare of the league." Ziegler never referred to Grant as an addict in his suspension statement, terming Grant's occasional intense usages as not constituting addiction level ("sporadic, sometimes 'bingeful' but never at an addictive level"). Still, he levied the second-longest drug-related suspension in NHL history against Grant.

The NHL's harsh approach in 1990 was at odds with emerging evidence that addiction is not a behaviour changed by dramatic punishment. Substance abuse has been called a set of self-destructive impulses that are out of control, yes, but the answer is not to stigmatize the user through public humiliation, particularly on the first instance. The current NHL policy involves a series of thresholds before the league imposes the kind of punishment Grant endured. The initial sanctions now involve fines, rehabilitation and counselling before a player can return. There is also leniency for players who seek help. The draconian sentence for Grant was a stark reminder that the league in 1990 was about punishment, not rehabilitation. In a culture with no effective drug policy, looking tough was more important than helping the players beat their addictive habits.

Grant:
We didn't think that I was going to get slapped on the fingers that hard. I would have been better off to have been caught rather than to have admitted it and sat through that hearing. I'd have gotten less punishment. Go back and see the guys who had gotten caught: they got maybe two or three games, a fine, no long suspensions, no nothing. It made zero sense

to me. So I was a little resentful for awhile. But there was nothing you could do about it at the time.

Ziegler did, however, offer an olive branch: if Grant stayed clean he might be restored to the Oilers after 60 games. In the months after the ban, Grant did act extremely contrite, and on February 4, 1991, Ziegler held another hearing and ruled that Grant could in fact return for Edmonton's 60th game of the 1990–91 season. He was allowed to immediately rejoin Edmonton's practices and to play for Cape Breton so that he could get himself into shape. Grant accelerated his NHL return by playing four games in six nights for the Oilers' farm club.

Grant:

The suspension was probably the most time I had ever spent in a gym up till then. I got to go to the gym every day, twice a day. Worked out a whole bunch. Got in about three weeks of practice. I was in mid-season shape when I started playing again, better than the way I started most seasons.

Playing his prep games in Cape Breton not only sharpened Grant's goaltending skills, it also helped him acquire a thicker skin. The hecklers in many arenas reminded him of the feedback he'd soon be getting around the NHL. In New Haven, Connecticut, for instance, Grant was taunted by a fan who held up a white substance in a plastic bag and a sign reading "PAY ME LATER."

Grant:

You'd see things or hear things, but you tried not to pay too much attention to them. They pay their money so they can say what they want. You can't let it get to you.

At the same time, when you're clean, your head's free to think about other things all of a sudden—which, as a goalie, is not always a bonus. You're supposed to be playing hockey and just paying attention to what's going on and just reacting. Then, all of a sudden now you have a clear head to look around and pay attention to things that you're not supposed to be paying attention to while you're playing. You now notice friends in the stands, you're looking around, you're not very focused.

The Oilers themselves certainly needed a boost from their legendary goalie as he made his return in New Jersey. They'd lost six of their previous seven contests and were sinking in the Smythe Division. To emphasize his return to sobriety, Grant took the nets wearing a blank white mask. It might also have been a statement about his tenuous position with Edmonton now that Bill Ranford had seemingly claimed the No. 1 job. With TSN's cameras sending his every move back to Canada, Grant's triumphant return to the Edmonton net on February 18 was truly an affair to remember. Fittingly enough, he pitched a shutout—the eighth of his career—blanking New Jersey by a 4–0 score. While the 27 saves were not the most he'd ever racked up in a shutout, Grant's superb comeback was still sweet redemption after his months away from the NHL. After the game, head coach John Muckler agreed, proclaiming, "You couldn't write a better script."

Grant:

I was a little bit sloppy and a little bit overactive at first. I reverted to what I would do as a kid, just pure reflexes. At the same time, it felt good to be back in there. To just play after all we'd been through was fun. Right out of the gate, a good start.

The return led to bigger and better things at first. The old Fuhr looked to be back, his body and mind seemingly unaffected by the wear and tear he'd gone through between 1987 and 1989, when dealing with his personal matters. Suddenly, Ranford was on the bench again and Grant was riding high, reclaiming the No.1 job down the stretch with a 6–4–3 record while putting up a solid 3.01 GAA and .897 save percentage. The Oilers were going to need him to return to form; the team was now a shadow of the roster that had won five Stanley Cups, with most players battling some combination of injury and age. Their .500 record in 80 games that year, however, was a remarkable turnaround considering they'd been 2–11–2 and last in the Campbell Conference on November 10.

Still, the once-mighty Oilers had been knocked down the Smythe Division pecking order with a third-place finish—their worst placing in the division since 1980–81. But the old magic came back in the first round against the highly favoured Calgary Flames. The fifth—and still most recent—playoff edition of the Battle of Alberta is best known for Theo Fleury's exultant goal celebration after beating Grant in overtime in Game 6 at Northlands. The goal sent the Flames into rapture and the series to another Game 7 in the fight between the provincial rivals. There the Oilers got their revenge when that match, too, ended in overtime—courtesy of Esa Tikkanen's hat trick that sank Calgary. Grant's performance during the series was arguably the best he had looked in three years, outplaying his counterpart Mike Vernon once more for old time's sake. It may even have been his best hockey in a playoff series yet.

It also left his backup in awe. "I was surprised how hard he pushes in practice," said Ranford later. "Even when they tell him to take a day off, usually he shows up. There's a lot of talk about who is the best, but Grant doesn't talk about it, he goes and proves it. He's a quiet guy who really doesn't thrive on attention at all. He doesn't go looking for the spotlight, but he ends up stealing it anyway with his play."

Grant kept up his hot streak in the next round against Gretzky's Kings, backstopping another upset of his old pal in six games before a hand injury caused him to come out of the last game in favour of Ranford. Whether the injured hand limited him or not, Fuhr couldn't sustain his tremendous play in the third round against Minnesota. Even Ranford could offer no refuge from the Cinderella North Stars: Minnesota brushed aside the Oilers in just five games, with Grant in net for the only Edmonton win. There would be no Stanley Cup in Edmonton in 1991, but there was a renewed sense of normalcy with Fuhr playing goal the old-fashioned way.

But not everything could return to normal: with owner Peter Pocklington hemorrhaging cash, and salaries for star players now soaring thanks to Gretzky, the surprising spring of 1991 proved a last hurrah for many in an Oiler uniform. Grant was among those stars of the Stanley Cup winners who would soon be on his way out of the City of Champions.

The man who'd once seemed to be an Oiler for life was about to embark on a remarkable journey to five other teams that would see him extend his legendary career and defy his critics.

GAME 8

John Muckler has always been a craggy, no-nonsense hockey man. He might also be one of the world's foremost experts on Grant Fuhr—a guy who's never been described as craggy or no-nonsense. In Edmonton, Muckler had helped transform the Oilers from a one-dimensional scoring machine to a defensively responsible team spearheaded by the best money goalie in hockey, No. 31. The bigger the game, the better Grant got. Now, as the head coach of the Buffalo Sabres in 1993, a continent away from his Edmonton roots, Muckler again made Grant his go-to guy in the post-season. And their chemistry was as potent as ever. "We've got the best playoff goalie in hockey," a smiling Muckler told reporters in the bowels of decrepit Boston Garden. The usually laconic Muckler was wearing that smile because his old standby had delivered yet again. Grant's fourth career playoff shutout, a shocking 4–0 waxing of the powerful Boston Bruins on their home ice, had put the underdog Sabres up two games to none in a series the experts claimed would be over in four straight for the Bruins.

In the Sabres dressing room, Grant tried to explain his extraordinary record in the games that meant the most. "I think I enjoy it more than anybody else," he told reporters. "Some guys seem to get a little bit uptight, a little bit nervous. I find it to be a little bit more of a challenge, because everybody picks their game up . . . I look forward to this time of year."

And the Sabres needed it. Despite the scoring exploits of Pat LaFontaine (148 points, 95 assists), Russian phenom Alexander Mogilny (127 points, 76 goals in 77 games) and Grant's former Memorial Cup nemesis Dale Hawerchuk (96 points, 80 assists), the Sabres of 1993 were not a team to be feared come playoff time. At the end of a mediocre season, they'd dropped their final seven games to wind up 23 points back of Boston in the Adams Division. To make matters worse, unlike typical Muckler teams, the Sabres were heavy on scoring but short on defensive talent—never a good formula heading into the meat grinder of the NHL playoffs.

In the Bruins the Sabres faced a team that had won 51 games and allowed 29 fewer goals than Buffalo. Led by Ray Bourque, Cam Neely and Adam Oates, and still featuring Grant's old partner Andy Moog in net, the Bruins were the trendy pick to emerge from the Wales Conference to play in the Stanley Cup final. But someone forgot to tell Grant Fuhr. When the lefty with the lightning hands was working his magic, none of the statistics mattered. After a surprising 5–4 OT win in Game 1 on a goal by Buffalo's Bob Sweeney, Grant was unbeatable in Game 2, pitching a shutout that silenced the Bruins' baying crowd. He made 34 saves, several of them of the spectacular variety. Bruins head coach Brian Sutter, who'd battled Grant as a player with St. Louis, was grudging in his praise. "If Fuhr's not standing on his ear, we win. He's a world-class goalie. What can you do?" The dramatic victory upped his playoff record to 76–32 while running his personal post-season record to 3–0 at Boston Garden.

No wonder Lafontaine gushed, "He's the best goalie I've ever faced, the best I've ever seen, and he's playing better now than he ever has. I'm glad he's on our side." Grant just shrugged. "This is my time of year," he told *SI*. "You play 84 games to get to the playoffs, so you might as well enjoy them once you get here."

The chances of Grant ever playing in another playoff game, let alone shutting out the mighty Bruins in the hostile bear pit of the Garden, had seemed remote as he headed to the 1990 Edmonton Oilers training camp. Bill Ranford's play had been wonderful in the previous spring's Cup run, and the Edmonton media were saying that, with Ranford on board, Grant was too much bother with his injuries and side issues. Still, Glen Sather preferred to wait before making a move. Grant's 60-game suspension had given Sather a temporary reprieve from the decision in the fall of 1990, but when the All-Star did finally return late in 1991 to play inspired hockey, Sather realized the time had come to make a decision on his goal-tending situation. Following Ranford's MVP performance at the Canada Cup in September, it seemed obvious who had a future in Edmonton and who would be moving on. Grant was still young at 28, but he had experienced a decade's worth of NHL hockey (includ-ing long post-seasons) and multiple injuries in that time—never mind the supposed toll from his party lifestyle. Four years younger, Ranford seemed so much more youthful than Fuhr in the eyes of fans and media. Plus, he had plenty of tread left on his tires, having been a starter for only two of his years in the NHL since 1986. And Ranford wouldn't need to be paid like Grant—a huge consider-ation in Peter Pocklington's financially stressed world.

Grant:

With Billy playing great you could see that the team was starting to change. The writing was on the wall. You just didn't know when it was going to happen, and I never really thought it would happen right away the next year. So I went to training camp, thought that camp was going fine, the team looked good and such. Never saw a trade coming yet.

Despite Grant's optimism, things were happening behind the scenes. As training camp loomed, Sather had received an offer he couldn't refuse from his old Calgary rival Cliff Fletcher, now the GM in Toronto. Looking to turn the Maple Leafs' fortunes around in the wake of owner Harold Ballard's death, Fletcher needed to make a bold move. While several teams had indicated interest in Grant, Toronto's package of players was the most attractive. (Plus it moved Grant out of the Western Conference and limited the chances of revenge—they'd all seen enough of Gretzky by that point.) So on September 19, 1991, the Maple Leafs acquired Fuhr from Edmonton along with Glenn Anderson and Craig Berube. In exchange, Fletcher surrendered Luke Richardson, Scott Thornton, Peter Ing and Vincent Damphousse.

Grant:

We were playing an exhibition game in Ottawa, and Glennie Anderson, Craig Berube and I had the day off and went golfing. We all got traded together while we were on the golf course. But if you had to go somewhere, Toronto was pretty cool. As a kid, I grew up as a Leafs fan, because you either had Toronto or Montreal on TV, and I used to love watching Johnny Bower and Terry Sawchuk play goal for the Leafs. So if I had to be traded, I thought it was a great place to go.

When asked how he could trade a goalie of Grant's calibre in the prime of his career, Sather admitted that the move was painful but necessary. "I'm sorry to see players like Grant and Glenn go, but I have to think in terms of the future of the Edmonton Oilers," he said. "We're getting some incredible young talent in return, and this team will be a force to be reckoned with for years to come."

Some were shocked that it was Cliff Fletcher who had nabbed Grant. He had, after all, spent many years trying to beat the nimble goalie and the Oilers in the Battle of Alberta. But it would not be the last time that a coach or general manager who had been victimized by Grant in the past would reach out to acquire him.

Grant:

I had a lot of respect for Cliff even though his teams in Calgary were always trying to beat us in Edmonton. Cliff was a nice man to deal with. Very straightforward, very honest, fun guy to be around. And he said flat out, "We don't have a good hockey team." I didn't realize at the time of the trade that it was quite as bad as it was, but he was right. It wasn't a very good hockey team. After my experience in Victoria and then Edmonton, I just didn't realize what a change it was to go from a really good team to a not very good team. For instance, being in Edmonton as long as I was, you never had to worry about reading off different defencemen. As soon as I got to Toronto it was a whole new group: now you've got to try and figure out what everybody's thinking.

Going from a five-time championship team to the sad-sack Leafs was like going from the NHL penthouse to its outhouse. In the final years under Ballard, the Leafs had become a bad joke, drifting as an organization according to the doddering owner's latest whims. Coaches and general managers came and went (at one point Ballard even promoted his public relations man, Gord Stellick, to be the team's general manager). After recycled GM Punch Imlach engineered the Lanny McDonald trade to Colorado in 1979, Toronto did not tally another winning record until 1992–93. They missed the playoffs six times, finished above fourth in their division only once, and won just two playoff series in those dozen years.

Lack of solid goaltending became one of many glaring weaknesses for the newly hired Fletcher to address in 1991. He knew better than almost anyone what he was getting in Grant, and Toronto arguably hadn't picked up a goalie with such a Hall of Fame resumé since Jacques Plante in 1970. Despite the recent bumps in the road, Grant was still a world-class goalie in Fletcher's eyes, and his gamble on Grant was a much-needed shot in the arm to the Leafs—who were coming off another disastrous season in which they finished with the second-worst record in the league. Furthermore, they'd already seen GM Floyd Smith waste their first-round pick on a misbegotten trade for the Devils' Tom Kurvers (New Jersey took Hall of Fame selection Scott Niedermayer with the pick).

Grant welcomed the challenge in Toronto with his usual wry sense of humour. When asked by reporters to compare the volume of shots he faced in Toronto to those in Edmonton, he quipped, "Well, at least it's a good way to break in equipment."

Toronto took some getting used to off the ice as well.

Grant:

It's completely different marketing-wise in Toronto than it is in Edmonton. The number of reporters and TV stations following you each and every day is amazing. There aren't many cities you can go where you get report cards for practice in the paper. I actually got a kick out of it.

Cushioning the blow of the trade to such a circus was the financial reward of moving from impecunious Edmonton to a team with money to spend. With salaries across the NHL jumping, Grant was finally able to cash in on his status as a top goalie.

Grant:

When I got to Toronto, Cliff wanted to sit down and do a new deal. And all of a sudden, I got a million dollars a year. After all the conflict in Edmonton with Glen [Sather] over money, this just happened so easily.

Though economic security had finally arrived, success on the ice was a little harder to find in Toronto. Pegged to reverse the Leafs' defensive woes in 1991–92, Grant did in fact lower the team's goals-against slightly, and in response, Toronto's record in the Norris Division improved by 10 points in the standings (from 57 to 67). Armed with his new deal, Grant played the work-horse role Fletcher had envisioned for him. Despite a series of nagging ailments, he was the clear No. 1 goalie, appearing in 65 games while posting a 3.66 GAA and a 25–33–2 record (these numbers despite a 12–1 loss in Pittsburgh in which coach Tom Watt left him in net for every goal). Those critiqu-ing the Leafs that season knew the problems did not lie with their newly acquired goalie, and that the fifth place finish in the division was due squarely to a puny scoring attack. The only team with a worse offence in 1991–92 was the expansion San Jose Sharks.

To remedy the non-existent offence, Fletcher engineered a dra-matic mid-season acquisition of his former Flames star Doug Gilmour in a 10-player deal with Calgary on January 2, 1992. The trade was the largest in NHL history, sending Gary Leeman and four others to Alberta for Gilmour, Jamie Macoun, Ric Nattress, Kent Manderville and Rick Wamsley. The boost from the leadership of Gilmour—who was about to become the most popular Leaf of the decade—improved the club after an awful start. But it was not enough to gain a berth in the post-season. Toronto still finished three points back of fourth-place Minnesota in the Norris, and for the first time since starting junior hockey, Grant was forced to miss out on his best time of the year.

Grant:

We still should have made the playoffs that year. That hurt a little bit, because it was my first miss of the post-season. That was a new experience. But you could see with Doug and the other new guys Cliff was bringing in that things were getting better.

It was a fun year. Andy and I roomed together for the first part of the year in Toronto, which is always entertaining. The drive to the rink every morning was a little longer than what I was used to in Edmonton. Twenty minutes to get you across the city in Edmonton, 20 minutes just to get you to Tim Horton's in Toronto.

The early end to the Maple Leafs' season allowed Grant to take his first major crack at playing pro golf, however. He teed it up at the Morningstar course in Parksville, British Columbia, to try to gain his tour playing card on the Canadian Professional Golf Tour (now the PGA Canada Tour). A five handicap at the time, Grant had visions of playing pro golf when his NHL career ended. Unfortunately, his first taste of the Tour was sour; he shot a two-day total of 174 to miss the cut.

Grant:

What bothered me was that I was nervous that first day on the Tour. I was surprised by that after all the golf I played, and the big hockey games. I felt better the second day, but by then it was too late. Still, it was fun to see how we stacked up against the guys who made a living at it. I learned a lot.

The Leafs would find resurgence under Gilmour's inspired leadership the following season. The future hadn't looked so bright for the team in decades—only Grant would not get to revel in the Toronto hockey renaissance. A series of injuries restricted his availability, and through the start of February he had played only 29 games for the reborn Leafs.

Grant:

I'd say that you're usually only 100 percent on the first day of training camp. That's it. After that there's always something that hurts. But you adjust to it and get used to it. I think my style contributed a bit to the injuries I had through those years: using strictly reflexes and throwing myself all over the place probably hurt the shoulder and knee ailments a bit.

The injuries opened a door in Toronto for rookie Felix Potvin and, eventually, closed a door for Grant. While he would begin 1992–93 as the definite No. 1 in the Toronto net, the stellar play of "Felix the Cat" during Fuhr's absences convinced Toronto it could do without the injury-plagued 30-year-old.

Grant remained confident he could regain the top spot in Toronto from Potvin in the long term. But, needing a winger to work with Gilmour, Fletcher decided to hedge his bets with Grant. Although the team was prospering on the ice, ownership complications in the wake of Harold Ballard's death were forcing Fletcher to consider players on big contracts. Simply put, Grant was making too much to be a backup goalie. Barely two years after Fletcher had acquired him, Grant was trade bait again.

Grant:

So just as we had learned the traffic part of getting around in Toronto, Cliff decided to make the deal with Buffalo in February of 1993. The Leafs were missing a couple pieces, and Cliff felt he could use me to get them from

Muck [John Muckler] in Buffalo. I knew they were getting better, and it was tough to leave just as the team was about to get back in the playoffs. As it turned out they went a long way that year, to the semi-finals. That was the year Wayne and the Kings beat them in that seven-game series.

In fact, in the 1993 playoffs, Toronto would barely miss on the team's first trip to the Stanley Cup final since 1967 (and a rematch with Montreal, whom they beat that year for their last Cup to date). But just as he'd played foil to Edmonton, Gretzky and his Kings scored a controversial win in seven games over Toronto in the Campbell Conference final. A non-call on a high stick by No. 99 on Gilmour remains a sore spot to this day for victory-starved Leafs fans.

As for Grant, the idea of No. 31 in blue and gold had piqued the interest of an old hockey connection. Sensing opportunity, John Muckler and the Buffalo Sabres pounced on the chance to shore up their own crease when they found out Grant was available. Buffalo acquired Fuhr on February 2, 1993, in what would, in retrospect, turn out to be an overpayment: Dave Andreychuk (who finished the year a 54-goal scorer thanks to 25 scores in 31 games playing alongside Gilmour), former all-star netminder Daren Puppa and a first rounder (respectable Swedish blueliner Kenny Jonsson) for Grant and a draft pick. But Muckler had coached Grant for eight years in the Oilers organization, and his word, more than anything else, convinced Buffalo GM Gerry Meehan the costly deal was worth the risk. "The price was high," Muckler said, "but we got what we needed."

Grant:

So, another trade. It was okay, because Muck was there. I'd played for him in Edmonton, which made it an easier transition. I lived in Toronto for the first two and a half, three weeks after the trade, drove back and forth to Buffalo, getting comfortable. But Buffalo had a good team—they actually had a really good team there. That helped the move as well.

While Andreychuk helped vault the Leafs to their best year in decades, Grant's impact wasn't as dramatic as the Sabres had envisioned. They went 12–16–4 in the rest of the season, with Grant sporting a 3.47 GAA and .891 save percentage in 28 appearances (while going 11–15–2). His backup, the Czech wonder Dominik Hasek, actually put up superior numbers, but he had no track record in the post-season.

Grant did play excellent hockey in stretches for his old friend Muckler. The Sabres were going to need it against the Bruins, their first-round opponent, who were a perfect 8–0 to finish the season, landing just behind Pittsburgh for the best record in the NHL's Eastern Conference. Buffalo, meanwhile, had not won a playoff series since 1983, and its fans had often been the victims of a post-season goaltending letdown despite reputable starters such as Tom Barrasso, Jacques Cloutier and Puppa. Fans were skeptical that this year, with an aging goalie—even one with Grant's pedigree—was going to be anything different.

But Grant had not earned his reputation as the best playoff goalie of his generation by accident. Summoning up his best form from the Edmonton days, he found his A game at just the right time for the showdown with first-place Boston in the Adams Division semi-final. If Grant needed added incentive, it was no doubt provided by the fact that he was facing his former stablemate Moog. (It ended up being the only playoff series in which they played every game against each other.) Grant's most vital contribution came in the Game 2 shutout in Boston: a 34-save contest in which Grant seemed to get into the heads of the Bruins shooters.

Even Boston's management was feeling the nerves as the series headed to the Aud in Buffalo. "On the basis of the first two games," said Boston president and general manager Harry Sinden, "I think we should win in Buffalo. But I thought we should win here, too." Sinden's caution was well-founded. Stabilized by Grant, the Sabres defeated the Bruins in overtime in Game 3 and 4, shutting the door on the Bruins' big shooters in extra time both nights. It was the Sabres' pugnacious forward Brad May's "May Day" goal (immortalized by Buffalo announcer Rick Jeanneret) that sealed the improbable sweep. Buffalo moved on to face the Montreal Canadiens in the Adams final, while the despondent Bruins dealt with their earliest playoff exit since 1987.

Then the old injury jinx cropped up again for Grant. A groin injury incurred in the Bruins series seemed to hamper him in the next round against Montreal, though no one else could resist the amazing karma of the Canadiens that spring either. The Habs, on their way to an unlikely Stanley Cup win behind their superb goalie Patrick Roy, won all four games against Buffalo by scores of 4–3—three of them ending in overtime (the Canadiens went a perfect 10–0 in OT that spring, a mark that may never be matched). While Grant lost the showdown with eventual Conn Smythe winner Roy, it seemed his performance had earned him a new home in western New York. Even more important, it had restored his confidence. Soon he began sporting a mask that had five Stanley Cups painted on it, one for each of his triumphs. "It's a reminder to me," Grant told writers. "But mostly it's a reminder to everyone else."

In addition, playing for Muckler, despite his reputation as a grumpy disciplinarian, was still a comfort zone for Grant, and his new teammates began looking to him as a conduit to their coach.

Grant:

The first full year I was in Buffalo was the first they brought in the new
NHLPA rules restricting how many hours you could be at the rink.
Muck's old-school. That rule was not going to be a big seller, and we
knew that. The first couple of days, we would practise for an hour,
skate for an hour, stretch for an hour. The guys were going down
with sore groins. They were getting tired. Guys I talked to, they were
just running out of gas three or four days into camp. Some of the players
thought that maybe somebody should mention to Muck that the guys
are falling apart.

Being the player with longest experience with Muck, they asked if I
minded having a word with him. I didn't have a problem with that, even
though I knew it wasn't going to be a very cheerful conversation. I said,
"I think the guys are done here." I got the quick "you're undermining my
authority" speech, and we were out of the office in about two minutes.

I was giving him feedback he didn't want to hear. Which I understood.
At the same time, Muck will listen. He won't tell you he's listening, and
he won't ever tell you that you were right. But he does listen, and he
was a good players' coach. He just would not ever let you know that
it was your idea.

Our practices got better after that. Just when you started to get too
comfortable, you'd have another one of those practice days, but it wasn't
every day. So maybe I had some effect.

Settled in Buffalo with future wife Candace after another divorce,
Grant sounded like he was planning to set down roots in the
community. "I figure I'll play five or seven more years," he told *SI*.
"I still have a few more people I want to torment." Once accli-
mated, he set about finding a place to indulge his other sporting
passion, golf. Getting onto the links helped him escape from the
pressures of his job in net. But that first summer, an incident on

the golf course would thrust him into uncomfortable territory as a national symbol of racial tension.

Grant had almost always shied away from addressing his place as a minority in a white-dominated sport. Generally he ignored the attention of those who called him a hero for all black hockey players while still recognizing the examples of Willie O'Ree and Mike Marson, who'd blazed a path before him.

Grant:

It was the same when people wanted to write stories about me being a black player. It was more of a story to them than it was to me. The same with the guys on the team: it was more an outside story than it was an inside story. Some of the US cities, if you go down to Buffalo, Washington, and some of the different cities, it was way more of a story. But in Canada, not so much.

Grant's colour, however, was an inescapable fact of his life at a time when political correctness was less prevalent than it is now. Some of his teammates in Edmonton had nicknamed him KoKo (after the WWF wrestler KoKo B. Ware), but Grant considered this part of the jocular humour of the dressing room, where everyone is teased. Other letters and comments from outside the room had not been as kind. Grant sloughed them off. Thanks to Bob and Betty, Grant saw the world as a place where character, not colour, defined you. While current standards would not tolerate the hazing Grant faced, he remains unaffected by the treatment and forgiving of those who teased him.

Grant:

I figured I could waste a lot of energy getting upset about things like that. But what was the point? At the end of the day I didn't want to be judged by anything but the way I played—what kind of teammate I was. So I left all that stuff to other people.

Unfortunately, there seemed no escaping race as a factor in his experience with the Transit Valley Country Club in the Buffalo suburb of Amherst, New York. And this time Grant would be less forgiving. Alex Mogilny, Dale Hawerchuk and several Sabre team officials were members of the club, and it seemed a natural place for Grant to obtain a membership—until he learned from second-hand sources that he would not be offered a place at Transit Valley. Grant was told the rejection was because he was black.

Grant:
A bunch of guys had joined Transit Valley. I applied there and got denied for no real reason. Then I found out what the reason was. That was kind of the first experience of that. It was like, "If that's the way they think, that's fine." Which other people there took a lot more seriously than I did. If they don't want you there, then you don't really want to be there.

In an interview shortly afterwards, Grant implied that his race might have been an issue in the decision, and the story hit the papers in Buffalo, generating a national firestorm. A statement from the club insisted Grant's attempt to gain membership was rejected due to "incomplete and incorrect" information on the application form. However, club officials refused to specify what that information was, citing that membership information was deemed confidential. The club received a huge backlash from the media and public, with accusations of racism and discrimination being levied against them. The fact the club had no black members stirred up the critics further. The week after the controversy erupted, the Transit Valley club was defaced when vandals broke onto the course and burned a swastika onto the 14th green. The club's office received a barrage of bomb threats, and threatening phone calls alleging the president was a member of the Ku Klux Klan.

There were also rumblings that the other Sabres personnel would cancel their memberships in protest if it were deemed racial bias had anything to do with Fuhr's rejection. Grant was appreciative of the support. He noted, "I've met a lot of nice members [from Transit Valley], and I feel bad for them. They all get painted with the same brush. That's unfortunate, because it's not all the members. That's what I'd like to emphasize." The club apologized and offered him a membership after all. The apology was accepted, but Grant eventually declined the offer after being admitted to the Fox Valley Club in nearby Lancaster, New York.

Grant:

They later came back and offered me a membership. I didn't think it was appropriate at that time: it was easier to just let bygones be bygones and stay where I was and play. Actually, we lived in a neighbourhood in Buffalo on the Country Club of Buffalo which, at that point, was a traditionally white golf club also. They're very friendly people. I had no problem going out there as a guest and playing. They wanted me to join and would have been happy to have me as a member.

Not surprisingly, the Transit Valley Country Club suspended its membership committee and formed a new committee to review the club's bylaws and constitution, specifically to incorporate anti-discriminatory language. With a statement that included the line "The Transit Valley Country Club does not discriminate based on race, sex, religion or ethnicity," it was obvious they were conducting heavy damage control.

Grant:

It stirred up some feelings in people in Buffalo. I actually wanted no part of it. Didn't really want to be part of the controversy. It was easier just to go to another golf club and play. Other people wanted it to go further along than it really needed to go, and I had no interest in doing that. I'd much rather just find another place where they'd rather have me play.

While Grant was a reluctant symbol of racial outrage, others took up his cause. Seeing the platform that Grant had as a black athlete in a white sport, they jumped on the incident. But Grant had always been unwilling to lead any crusades. When Toronto Maple Leafs owner Harold Ballard had passed on Grant in the 1981 draft to select Jim Benning, Leafs legend Johnny Bower (then a scout for the team) said, "He was my number one choice. But the organization felt that we couldn't draft a black player at that time. I told the team that we would regret it if we don't choose him. And I stand by it to this day." Ironically, Grant was a Leafs fan and would willingly play for Toronto after Ballard died, but he never criticized the Maple Leafs for the decision.

Then in 1988, Bob White, a coach and mentor to many black athletes in Montreal, used Grant to make a point about racial discrimination in Canada. "If Fuhr had been born in Quebec, he might not have made it to the NHL," White says. "You can be recruited with a mask on, like Grant Fuhr. He was lucky he was out west, outside of Quebec. And it's good he wears the mask." A spokesman for the National Institute Against Prejudice and Violence said Fuhr was an easy target for prejudice. "They pick an acceptable target, someone they think is okay to treat as a non-person."

Grant:

It wasn't like it was a crisis for me. My parents taught me that race doesn't define you as a person. My parents had always brought me up that everybody's the same. When you play hockey, you're not black or white. A person on the street's another person on the street. Everybody puts their pants on the same; everybody puts shirts on the same. You treat everybody the same. Back home, I think there were two other black kids at school—a couple of brothers, Donovan and Percy Whitaker— that was it. There were some Native kids in the school, and I played ball with and hockey with them. Everybody knew you were either a hockey player, or ball player, or you were one of the kids. There was never anything about race.

Still, working in America for the first time was an illuminating experience for the product of sleepy Spruce Grove, Alberta.

Grant:

It was also my first experience playing in the States. It was kind of an eye-opener that, okay, everything you see on TV is actually true. It exists. The first thing I really noticed was when a friend from Edmonton had come down: we were sitting in a restaurant having breakfast, and he'd ordered brown toast. In Canada, you order brown toast, everybody knows you want whole wheat. Everybody got their breakfast and finished for half an hour, he hadn't gotten his breakfast yet. There was this older black lady who was serving us, she didn't take the order of brown toast very well. We had no idea. Nobody even thought twice about it.

All of a sudden, you knew you were in a different element. Words had to be chosen a little more carefully. What's status quo at home is not status quo there. We were a little more careful about those things when we got to Buffalo.

In my opinion, it's more an American deal that race means something—

it means more there. Fortunately in the sports world, you're an athlete first and foremost. Society should be more that way.

Though Grant is idolized first and foremost for his on-ice achievements by goalies of all backgrounds, young black players who followed him to the NHL, such as Jarome Iginla (from St. Albert, Alberta) and Fred Brathwaite, made a point of acknowledging his importance as a role model.

Grant:

Fred called me when he came up in Edmonton. He wanted to ask my permission to wear No. 31 with the Oilers. I said it was okay. I knew Jarome from when he was four. His uncle was the manager and he was the bat boy on our team. Jarome was always a good pro. He still puts the time in, puts the effort in, he's good with the kids and that's what you really love to see.

————

After his playoff heroics for Buffalo in 1993, Grant thought he had found a place where he could become comfortable in the starter's role for awhile. For a third time, however, he was about to find himself playing the warm-up act to a younger player—this time, to one who would eventually win a stunning six Vezina trophies. In the 1992 off-season, the Sabres had made a trade for Czech phenom Dominik Hasek, soon to be known as "The Dominator."

Grant:

Dom had started to play well and was starting to make his presence known. I had seen him from the Canada Cup in 1987 when he almost beat us singlehandedly for the Czechs. You knew Dom was good from that game alone. There was no question. Dom was great in Chicago: I remember that great breakaway save he made on Mario [Lemieux] in the 1992 playoffs. It's just the Blackhawks had Eddie Belfour. Jimmy Waite was there; Greg Millen was there. Dom didn't have the opportunity to play, and they had a lack of coaching. It just didn't fit. He got shipped to the Sabres in a trade for almost nothing, and was already in Buffalo when I got there. Bet Chicago wishes it could have that one back.

As was often the case, Grant's approach to conditioning didn't help his case as the starter. In 1993–94, Grant came to his first full Buffalo camp well above the weight the Sabres wanted, exasperating Muckler. "One thing that maybe Grant doesn't realize is that he's not 20 years old anymore, he's 30 years old," sniffed his coach. "It takes a little bit longer to get the conditioning up. He knows that he's going to pay the price. And we'll get him in shape."

Grant was still of the opinion that he knew best how to get Grant Fuhr ready to play, however. But as Muckler predicted, the price for carrying excess weight into the season was recurring troubles with Grant's ever-worsening knees. While Grant attempted to get himself back to playing shape, the lithe Hasek, a training fanatic, stole the spotlight and the No. 1 job en route to the first of his Vezina Trophy seasons. The limber Czech was also a runner-up for the Hart Trophy that year. Even though Grant enjoyed sharing a Jennings Trophy with Hasek for the league's lowest team GAA, his numbers that season were mediocre by his own standards—a 13–12–3 record with a bloated 3.68 GAA and .883 save percentage. Hasek, meanwhile, went 30–20–6 in 58 appearances, and had a stunning GAA of 1.95 (the lowest mark in three decades) with seven shutouts and a .930 save percentage (a record at the time). Even harder for Grant to swallow, Hasek started for Buffalo come playoff time and played brilliantly in a seven-game opening-round defeat at the hands of the New Jersey Devils.

Grant:

I got to play for a year in front of him, and shared the job the second year. I got to see him play every day. Phenomenal work ethic. Every shot meant something even in practice. He took it to another level, which was great to watch. He understood the game better than most guys I played with. He was a student of it and wanted to know certain things. He was actually a lot of fun to play with: in fact, he reminds me of [Miikka] Kiprusoff a little. Kipper and Dom would be guys who had the athletic style—not the pure butterfly. Kipper was a little more in control than Dom. Even though he looked like he was all over the place, he was in pretty good control. You'd see him make a lot of second and third saves that most guys couldn't get.

Although Hasek's extraordinary rise and starring role in the playoffs made Grant feel expendable after the season, decisions about Grant's future weren't uppermost in anyone's mind—at least not right away. In September 1994, the NHL owners invoked their first player lockout, a labour stoppage that stretched until February 1995. During the lockout, commissioner Gary Bettman prohibited teams from making trades or signing players. But when hockey finally started again, the Sabres had a problem to face: they couldn't afford to pay two starting goalies the market value created by the new collective agreement. In the past, salaries and bonuses had typically been tied to team goals. But with salaries shooting upward in this new NHL economy, the criteria for getting paid was slowly morphing, and goalies were now being judged more on individual statistics than on wins or losses.

Grant:

You had to get your numbers down now. Save percentage. Goals against average. I still said that the only thing that mattered was whether you won or lost, but now all of a sudden, come contract time, everybody wanted numbers. You could plead your case like, "I won X number of games, lost X number of games," and they'd sit there and go, "Well, look at the other numbers you have." It didn't matter. "Would you prefer me to have great numbers and split the wins and losses?" "That's not important." Growing up through sports, I thought the winners usually get rewarded, the losers don't. I think it's still important. But this was a different philosophy entering the game at that point.

Adjusting to the new reality—and the spiking salaries—Grant drove himself to be in better shape to extend his career. As play resumed in 1995, he began using aqua aerobics as a way to stay fit, even though he couldn't swim. As Grant explained to the late Jim Kelley of the *Buffalo News* about his workout regimen: "I had to decide if I still wanted to play in the National Hockey League and, if I did, at what level. Once I decided that I did want to keep playing, I knew I had to do something to make sure that I could. . . . There are some people in Buffalo and in the organization that feel they made a mistake in getting me," he added. "I want to prove them wrong."

Still, John Muckler could see which Sabre goalie had a bit less wear (Hasek was 30 to Grant's 32) and the better numbers. It made for an uncomfortable dilemma. "Dominik was the best goalkeeper in the NHL last season," explained Muckler as the Sabres assembled following the lockout. "Grant Fuhr's history tells you he's a Hall of Famer, and the way he's played in camp shows he can still be a No. 1 goalie."

Grant:
You knew he was younger than I was. He was going to play most of the games. You knew the transition's going to happen at some point. He had

signed a long-term deal (at three years/$8 million) so he wasn't about to sit
on the bench. Neither was I. When you head to the bench as No. 2 goalie,
you've kind of surrendered. I wasn't ready to surrender just yet.

Even so, Grant saw the future clearly. "If I'm a betting person,
I'd bet I'm not here by training camp," Fuhr told the *Buffalo News.*
"That's just my assessment of the situation. Economics say I won't
be here next year. That's a goaltender for you. Always aware of
where players stand, whether on the ice or amid the salary structure. They've got to sign 17 guys or so over the next year and a
half, two years. That doesn't bode well for somebody that's 32 and
making $2 million a year. So reality says I'll be moving."

Reporters asked him if he might be ready to give up hockey if
he got his pro golf card that summer. "I'd look at it," Fuhr said. "I
don't know if I'd do it, but I'd look at it. Aw, I know I'd put in one
more year [of hockey]. I may be a goalie, but I'm not dumb."

In his own defence, Grant noted for the press that while Buffalo
seemed a little rich in goal, the Sabres were not actually a deep
team at the position. A second dependable goalie was not an
extravagance—as his time in Edmonton had demonstrated more
than once. Muckler could see the value, and wanted to keep Grant,
but it would have to be at a lower price.

Grant:

My contract was coming up, and Muck called me in and said, "I can sign
a deal with you as a backup, and you can have as long-term a deal as
you'd like." I probably could have gotten a four- or five-year term as a
backup. Or I could decide to maybe go somewhere else and play. They
gave me the option. I wasn't ready to be a backup, so I said, "Well, if you
can move me somewhere to play, I'll try that."

When Grant stumbled out of the gate in the lockout-shortened 1994–95 season, playing just three games and allowing 12 goals, the decision to send him elsewhere in search of a starting job became academic. On February 14, Buffalo sent him to play with his old pal Wayne Gretzky in Los Angeles. The deal was Grant for Alexei Zhitnik, Robb Stauber and Grant's former Edmonton teammate Charlie Huddy. Once again it was an overpayment by a team hoping to catch some of the old Oilers magic from Grant. It was also a reflection of the respect his name commanded despite a bumpy few years.

The trade did give the Kings two of the more easy-going goalies in the league, with Grant and Kelly Hrudey. Kings defenceman Sean O'Donnell said that no team in the history of the league ever had two more outwardly mellow netminders.

Grant:

They shipped me to L.A., and Kelly Hrudey was having a career year there. The rest I wasn't quite sure about, other than Gretz and a lot of former Oilers were there. I said, "Let's go down there and see what happens." I didn't play very much the first little while. The first couple of games that I did play, I was horrible. Probably a little disinterested, knowing that you'd gone from somewhere where you're not going to play to somewhere else where you're not going to play. I sat with [Kings coach] Barry Melrose, and he said, "Your job's to help the young guys develop." Okay, fine. I didn't play much for a while, but my golf swing got a lot better.

"When we made the trade, he was in Buffalo and he hadn't been playing a lot," Kings general manager Sam McMaster told the *L.A. Times* after Grant had settled in. "When he got here, I don't think he was game-sharp and that just compounded the situation.

If he had played the way he's playing [now], it would have been a different situation . . ."

For Hrudey, having Grant as his competition was uncomfortable. "It was almost unfair for us to compete. In retrospect, you could see he was having a crisis of confidence. It was obvious to us things hadn't gone well in Buffalo. His game wasn't great; we weren't great. I was concerned if he could get back to that level."

Grant:

By the last 10 or 12 games, they had fired Melrose, and Rogie Vachon gave me an opportunity to play, because we were pretty much out of the playoff picture at that point. I started to play better, better and better. I got my confidence back. So I knew I could still do it. The question was what role was there with the Kings? They said they wanted me—but for what?

I decided not to re-sign in L.A. I definitely had already decided that L.A. wasn't going to be a good fit. They were going in a different direction. Kelly had had a great year, so it was going to be another one of those situations where you don't know if you're going to play or not. After that, I was sitting at home, trying to figure out where we were going.

That was the lowest ebb of Grant's career. In the summer of 1995 he was back at home in Edmonton, without a team, without a fitting conclusion to a great career. Few, including the man himself, could have foreseen the dramatic turnaround that lay ahead.

GAME 9

Grant Fuhr had seen an oncoming forward bent on mayhem hundreds of times in his 15 NHL seasons. It came with the territory of the blue paint. But the outcome of the scrum in front of the St. Louis net in Game 2 of the 1996 Western Conference semi-final would be anything but routine. With a possible sixth Stanley Cup ring in sight that spring, Grant had staked the Blues to a 1–0 games lead in their playoff series against Toronto. Eight minutes into the second contest, however, agitator Nick Kypreos of the Maple Leafs crashed Grant's net in search of the puck. The Blues defenceman, six-foot-five Chris Pronger, quickly moved to clear Kypreos from the crease, using his bruising physical style to shove the Maple Leafs forward.

Grant:

It was actually just a routine shot from the side that kind of got knocked into the front of the net. There was a little bit of a scramble. I got down to cover up the puck. There was the usual push-and-shove, push-and-shove with Kypreos and Prongs that you get all the time in the playoffs. Next thing you know, Kypreos kind of turned and leaned over and fell on my leg, which just happened to be in a vulnerable spot. I had somebody's stick or leg caught under my leg, so it couldn't get flat. I knew as soon as he landed on it something was wrong, but I had no idea what. I'd had Timmy Kerr fall on me before that, a lot bigger than Nick was. But this was different. We weren't very happy for a couple of months afterwards.

That would be an understatment. St. Louis coach Mike Keenan outright accused Kypreos, a journeyman tough guy, of attempting to injure his star goalie, who now had a torn anterior cruciate ligament (ACL), a torn medial collateral ligament (MCL) and a torn meniscus as a result of the play. "[Kypreos] deliberately tried to make contact with [Fuhr]," Keenan claimed after the game. "He wasn't pushed into him as everybody thought he had been. In fact, our defenceman tried to push him away from the goaltender. But he made direct contact, and it resulted in a season-ending injury to a very key player on our team. It's unfortunate that he decided . . . maybe his coach did, I don't know . . . to take out a premier player on our team. There's no excuse for it." Years later, Keenan was no less certain. "Absolutely he fell on him," he recalls. "Every time I see the tape of the play I come to the same conclusion."

"He didn't fall on him. He jumped on him," says Blues teammate Geoff Courtnall. "On purpose. Grant had the puck in the crease and he tore out his knee. Of course, I can't say I haven't ever hit a goalie, either."

Grant was no less steamed when he finally talked to reporters after the game about the slo-mo Kypreos tumble. "If a guy drives the net I have no problem with that. It's a good, honest play. But if there's a pileup and a guy jumps on a goalie, that's a joke. The job is tough enough trying to dodge those linebackers bumping into you left and right. There's no mystery what Kypreos was thinking . . . If I get run into again I'm taking someone with me. I lost one knee. I'll take a head if it happens again."

The loss of Fuhr for the rest of the playoffs (and who knew how long into the next season) was a major blow for both Grant and the Blues. With his old Oilers teammate Wayne Gretzky now on board to join Brett Hull and the defensive duo of Pronger and Al MacInnis, there had been hope—and a considerable economic stake—in a sustained run at a first Cup in St. Louis. "Here's the thing," recalls Courtnall. "That year we had a great team. Wayne was there. Hully was there. Pronger was great. We were deep. Mike had put together a really good team. We had a chance. Without Grant we took Detroit to overtime in the seventh game, and I think if he's healthy it would have made the difference, we win that series and maybe go the whole way."

Considering the acrobatic, flexible nature of Grant's goaltending style and his age (34), a surgically reconstructed knee raised major doubts about his ability to continue what he'd built in 1995–96. The Fuhr/Kypreos crash became the biggest story in the early rounds of the 1996 NHL playoffs.

The fact that Grant was in a position to be a major storyline in an NHL playoff season might have come as a surprise to many hockey observers just a year earlier. After reaching rock bottom in Los Angeles the previous summer, when Grant had resolved not to sign again with the Kings, it had seemed that the injury-plagued goalie was now a scrap-heap option, washed-up and nothing more than backup material. But he and his agent Mike Barnett believed there was still a place where Grant could carry the load as a No. 1 starter. "It was a matter of finding the right place for him," says Barnett. "There was still plenty left in the tank as far as I was concerned."

Grant:

I wanted to go home to Edmonton that summer, just sit and weigh my options. Mike Barnett thought he could get me an offer to be a No. 1 guy somewhere. I just told him I wanted to see what offers there are, if any. At that time, Mike Keenan was trading everybody in St. Louis. He had decided to trade Curtis Joseph to Edmonton. Keenan was in Edmonton for the 1995 draft, and I remember him calling me, saying, "If I gave you a million dollars, would you come to St. Louis and play?" "Yeah." That's a no-brainer of an idea. He says, "Do you have a fax?" I'm like, "Yeah." "I'm going to fax you a contract." "Okay." Sat and waited. Sure enough, he faxed me a contract for a million bucks a year. That's how I ended up going to St. Louis.

With Keenan heading into the second season of a three-year tenure in the Gateway City, the Blues' roster was changing rapidly. He wanted to win, and he wanted to win now. The former Philadelphia Flyers and New York Rangers coach had overhauled the look of the Blues by signing free-agent veterans such as Shayne Corson, Dale Hawerchuk, Brian Noonan and Geoff Courtnall. Keenan had also traded the Blues' beloved power forward Brendan Shanahan to Hartford for a still-green defenceman named Chris Pronger. He then planned to shuttle Joseph (who was a contract holdout) to Grant's former team in Edmonton for two first-round picks.

With Cujo gone, the door would suddenly be open for Grant to grab the job as Keenan's No. 1 starter. The two men were hardly strangers: Keenan had not only coached Fuhr in the 1987 Canada Cup but, as an opposing coach, had seen what Grant was capable of when his Flyers had been beaten in two Cup final meetings with the Oilers. "At the top of his game he was the best goalie in the world," says Keenan. "I'd seen it first-hand." The only question remaining was what was left in that body and mind. Could Grant do it again?

The answer came when Keenan, visiting in New York City in the summer of 1995, had a chance encounter with Wayne Gretzky and his wife, Janet. "I was sitting having as drink at an outside patio when, all of a sudden, a taxi pulls up to a stop and out jumps Wayne," recalls Keenan. "I asked him if he could stop for a drink. He says, I'll be back in an hour. Sure enough, he and Janet show up an hour later." Over a glass of wine, a curious Keenan asked the Gretzkys whether there was anything left in Fuhr. Absolutely, Wayne and Janet chimed in. He just needs a little confidence right now, said No. 99. He's just waiting for another chance. In the mercurial Keenan, Fuhr had found the believer he needed to jump-start his illustrious career.

Back in St. Louis, Keenan's long-simmering contract squabble with Curtis Joseph had led to the seemingly locked-in goalie holding out. While Keenan was not afraid to spend his owner's money, he dug in on Joseph. Rather than acquiesce to his star goalie, Keenan cobbled together a replacement plan in the form of a couple of once highly regarded netminders. Grant and Jon Casey would take Cujo's place while Joseph was dealt to Edmonton in August of '95 (where he continued to hold out until he got a deal he liked in 1996). To justify the trade, Keenan explained to reporters that Joseph was out of shape, but when the decision was announced, most thought it was more impulsive "Mad Mike" than Iron Mike. The hockey world scoffed at the idea that a washed-up Grant Fuhr was the answer to anything—let alone a substitute for Joseph. But after the endorsement from Gretzky, Keenan was defiant as usual. Fuhr was going to be his man and lead the Blues into the playoffs.

Grant soon discovered that he was walking into a hornet's nest.

Grant:

I didn't realize that Curtis had just come off being the most popular player in St. Louis. I had missed that news somewhere along the way. I got to

St. Louis, and we're already behind the eight ball. The most popular guy on the team had gotten shipped out, because Mike said he wasn't in good enough shape. Turns out Curtis was in better shape than I was.

I got to training camp there in what I thought was okay shape for me. I was about 212. I thought I could do what I always did: play myself into shape. Mike wanted to see it a little bit differently. Mike had played with the scale a little bit, so the numbers he reported were a little different.

"The truth is Grant showed up maybe 20 pounds overweight, marked his weight down on the sheet and then went up to his room," says Geoff Courtnall. "Keenan looked at the weight he'd marked down and said, 'Go get Fuhrsie.' I was right there. They went and got him out of his hotel room and weighed him again. And Keenan sent him home and told him when he gets in shape he can come back. But you know, it probably revitalized his career from that point."

Keenan reported that Fuhr had come in at 219 pounds and had failed to finish the VO2 bike-riding segment of the pre-season physical exam. Grant offered reasons for the failure: his left knee had bone spurs that prevented him from taking the bike test, and the pins inserted surgically in both his shoulders ruled out the military-style bench press. Keenan was unmoved and suspended his newly acquired saviour. People around the Blues who'd been counting on a chiselled Grant Fuhr to lead their team took a big gulp. "Anyone who tells you they weren't in a panic at that point is a lying sack of s——," Blues forward Brett Hull told *SI*.

Grant:

I got shipped home after a week and decided I was just going to go play golf. When I flew home to Edmonton, a friend picked me up. We went over to the university hospital to get weighed. I mysteriously lost seven pounds on the flight home. There was something a little amok. Which was fine; it was Mike's way of saying hello.

While I was suspended I went to Boston to play in a golf tournament. Meanwhile, the rest of the guys just happened to be playing an exhibition game in Boston, and Mike found out about it. My fault for being out golfing instead of being back at camp. I got told that I should get back to St. Louis and be ready to play. I got back and we had a conversation. "I won't say anything bad about you, if you don't say anything bad about me." It was little late: I'd already been getting roasted in the paper for a week. There wasn't much more bad that could be said about me.

Mike says, "Here's how it's going to work. Play, and I'll tell you when to stop." I'm like, "Okay." At Christmas it was, "You tired?" I'm like, "Nope." "Good. Just play." I'm like, "Okay." February: "Are you tired?" "Nope." "Fine. Just play."

Rather than risking Keenan's ire again, Grant decided he might try to be more vigilant about his physical conditioning. Blues trainer Ray Barile hooked him up with famed St. Louis–based track and field trainer Bobby Kersee, whose wife Jackie Joyner-Kersee was the world record holder in the heptathlon at the time. Kersee, who had a reputation as a taskmaster, took one look at the tires around Grant's waist and designed a stretching and conditioning program for him. He also issued a fatwa on Grant's diet of junk food, urging him to eat healthier.

Grant:

I was in the habit of eating munchies late at night in front of the TV. All that had to go. I wasn't a fanatic about it: we still put cream in my coffee in the morning. I still ate a burger once in awhile. But the rest of the time it was good stuff. I became good friends with Bobby, because he would push, and push, and push—which some days you needed. Some days it just hurt, and it wasn't very much fun, and it was pretty easy to lose the focus on what you're trying to do. He made it fun. Or as fun as that kind of stuff can be.

Pretty soon, Keenan was boasting about Grant's body fat level dropping almost as fast as his goals against average. But it wasn't all good news. Grant's pre-season home debut went awry as the rusty goalie allowed five goals on just 12 shots before being yanked in the second period for Bruce Racine—to the cheers of fans at the Kiel Center. But the Blues coach/GM and his streamlined goalie got the last laugh. Setting records for goalie activity, Grant appeared in 79 games that season, all but three of the Blues' contests that year. If it weren't for a strained knee in a game against the Wings on March 31, he could conceivably have started every single game for St. Louis that year—a feat never accomplished in the 82-game NHL. He broke the NHL record for consecutive games started within one season by going 76 straight (prior to that the record had been 70, last accomplished in 1963–64 by the Bruins' Eddie Johnston). It was the comeback effort of the decade, with Grant posting career bests in just about every category, topping his old save percentage by four-tenths with a .903 mark and posting his first sub-3.00 GAA (a 2.87 average in the 79-game haul). He also led the league in shots faced (2,157) and saves (1,948). "When I coached Grant in St. Louis he was an absolute workhorse [for us]," Keenan recalls. "I won't say I expected him to play every game, but I knew he could handle the work. He was a great athlete who was able to master his position as a goaltender with incredible stamina, reflexes and instincts for the position."

Much of this was accomplished in front of a putrid offence, making every goal Grant allowed a crucial one. To win the Stanley Cup, Keenan knew he needed more than a stingy defence. In

March, the Blues struggling offence got a jolt when Keenan pried Wayne Gretzky out of L.A. with a massive trade (when the Maple Leafs declined to acquire him). Gretzky joined Grant and fellow Edmonton alumni Glenn Anderson, Charlie Huddy and Craig MacTavish on the Blues. The acquisition of "The Great One" was necessary for St. Louis to make the playoffs, as their vaunted offensive talent hit a major power outage in 1995–96, scoring just 219 times (43 of those goals provided by Brett Hull alone). Only the Devils and Senators scored fewer. In fact, eight of the 10 non-playoff teams produced more goals than the Blues that year. Still, with 80 points they snuck in past a few teams to claim the fifth seed in the tightly bunched Western Conference.

By that point, Grant had won over his coaches and teammates. "Almost every night he's been one of our top players," Blues assistant coach Bob Berry told reporters. "We used to sit on the bench and say, 'Damn, did you see that save?'" said St. Louis defenceman Al MacInnis, Grant's former rival in Calgary. Without Grant, said Brett Hull, "We'd have won five games, maybe seven, honest to god." In spite of the heroics, Grant finished sixth in Vezina voting. He also finished sixth in the Hart Trophy contest. Curiously, his Hart vote total (taken by the media) ranked him ahead of all five goalies who'd finished ahead of him in the Vezina vote (according to the GMs who voted).

Grant:
You can't put too much attention in that sort of thing. Maybe I'd been a little harder on general managers than on the media by that point. Who knows? It's all good now.

In Game 1 of the Blues' Western Conference opening series with Toronto at Maple Leaf Gardens, Grant marked his return to playoff hockey after a three-year absence with a 31-save performance. (He was beaten only by an old nemesis and teammate, Doug Gilmour, on a power play.) Based on his dominating performance in front of a national TV audience on *Hockey Night in Canada*, Grant looked ready to supply championship goaltending to a team loaded with stars—not a team that had just finished with a mediocre 80-point season. With Gretzky and Hull supplying offence while Grant made like a brick wall, there was hope entering Game 2. Enter Kypreos and the dying swan dive. The good vibes surrounding Grant and the Blues snapped along with Grant's ACL and MCL when the Leafs forward fell on his leg during Game 2 of the opening round.

Grant:

I was pretty mad at Nick for a while. Now we laugh about it when we see each other. These things happen in the playoffs. He was just trying to help his team, not hurt me. Anyhow, I went back to St. Louis and they took an MRI of the knee. Not so good. I decided that, okay, the ACL's gone. The MCL's gone. If I put a brace on, can it work?

For Keenan—still livid at Kypreos and Toronto coach Pat Burns—even a remote chance to keep his goalie in the net was worth exploring. "We're going to explore every possibility—if Grant wants us to, and I think he does," Keenan told reporters.

Grant:

I went out to one morning skate and thought, "Well, it's not hurting a whole lot." Standing there, I was fine. I was like, "Maybe I can do this." As soon as I went down, though, we were stuck. Didn't realize you actually have to have ligaments to get back up. The knee bent in a funny spot and it wouldn't unbend. No stability, nothing to push on—that was a problem.

So I had to have a lovely four-and-a-half-hour surgery. I'd never had a major surgery before this. It had just been minor stuff, cleaning things up. In those days, they'd do an ACL repair and an MCL repair in separate surgeries. But I had an ACL, MCL and meniscus completely done at once. Which, for the two days afterwards, I could feel in its entirety. It had my undivided attention.

With Jon Casey replacing Grant in net, the Blues subdued Toronto in six games, but then fell in seven to Detroit. Game 7 went to double OT before Steve Yzerman's famous long shot beat Casey and sent Detroit to the next round. It was one of the most dramatic goals in playoff history, and the heartbreaking finish only made Grant's knee feel worse. There was just one way to ease the pain.

Grant:

I decided I was going to make it back, and told them I wanted to make it back for training camp. They said, maybe by Christmas, but I wanted to be back before that. I never would've gotten back as soon without Bob Kersee. Not a chance. Maybe I might not have gotten back at all. Bob pushed the flexibility and strength, and every time you felt like you were hitting a wall, he would push you through that wall. Then you'd sit there and shake your head trying to figure out what happened.

I think that the pain was part of it. Every time you thought you got to a certain point, he'd take it away from you so there was nothing to focus on, and you'd have to go back to the start and push again. The way he pushed Jackie, though—I think I got the lighter end of the deal. I could leave him there at the end of the day. To train with him, one, it was a lot of fun; two, it was a learning experience to see what he and Jackie went through every day for her to be best at what she did.

Grant arrived at Blues camp in September 1996 ready to prove that his rehabilitation was complete. Typically, he downplayed the pain and anxiety of the summer's gruelling work with Bob Kersee. An insouciant Grant told the Blues beat reporters, "It's been a four-month vacation. I think it's been long enough." Keenan was hopeful but knew the history of recovery from such knee problems. "I knew if anyone could do it, it would be Grant. But at his age I knew there were no guarantees."

Grant:

I had decided the first day of camp I was going to skate. I went to kneel down and felt something sharp in my knee and was like, "That's not going to work." One of the heads of a screw was kind of sticking out a bit in the front of the kneecap. We had to run over to the doctor's to get that taken out. He kind of opened it up, took a Black & Decker drill out and just backed out the screw. Yeah. They just put a little local freezing in it. I was kind of hoping for something advanced and elaborate, but he just backed it out like [it was in] a piece of wood, which I didn't find very amusing.

With the screw fixed and the knee stable, Grant launched into a remarkable comeback that made his Iron Man show the previous season look pedestrian. Showing the resilience that defined his career, Fuhr recovered from what could have been a career-ending injury to post a nearly identically superb season. Ironically, 1996–97 was to be Grant's first—and last—year free of major health woes since the Canada Cup/Stanley Cup double in 1987–88. Playing with renewed confidence, he was again a workhorse for Keenan, appearing in a league-high 73 games while posting a career best 2.72 GAA. "Nothing Grant does surprises me," remarked Gretzky, who had left the Blues for the New York Rangers as a free agent that summer. "They counted him out in Edmonton, in Toronto, in Buffalo and in

Los Angeles. But he came back. I knew if there was any way possible for him to come back from that surgery last spring, Grant
was the one person who could do it. That's why he's so great in
goal; he never gives up. He thrives on proving people who say
he's finished wrong. He's a special player. Some might say he's
the comeback player of the year. To me, Grant Fuhr has been
counted out so many times that he should be the comeback player
of the decade."

Grant, meanwhile, was his laconic self about all the fuss. "I
think sometimes people lose sight of the fact that it is a game,
and they take it too serious," he told reporters. "If you happen to
give up a goal, you're not going to die from it. If you just relax,
enjoy it and remember it's a game, you can survive in this game
a long time."

With his knee healthy, Grant was left alone by Keenan, who was
now coming under pressure himself for his dramatic and costly
moves—ones that hadn't gotten St. Louis to the promised land. He
also had his hands full with some of his other players, such as the
famously irascible Brett Hull.

Grant:

Mike just left me alone and let me play, which was awesome. He was too
busy with Hully; he and Hully were having their feud. Brett and I were at
the rink together every day, played golf together every day. He had his own
theories on the world at that point, Mike had his, and they were not in the
same universe. I sat beside Al MacInnis, who I played against all the time
when I was in Edmonton, and we looked at each other and said, "It's not
like that in Calgary and it certainly wasn't like this in Edmonton." Mike and
Brett would yell at each other, but it kept life pretty entertaining. My best
Hully story is probably when he and Mike had an argument one night in
the middle of a game. Hully stomped into Mike's office between periods

and you could hear Hully kick his desk, and Hully came limping back out
screaming, thinking he'd broken his foot in between periods of the game.

Making Grant's successful return particularly special was his
ability to adapt his game to a changing NHL. The freewheeling
league he joined as a rookie in Edmonton was quickly morphing
into a league dominated by defence and coaches obsessed with
video. The average goals-per-game in the league was dropping
quickly from a peak of eight in the early '80s to under six.
Equipment changes were also making life very different for
goalies brought up in an earlier era: butterfly coaches such as
Francois Allaire (and his prized pupil Patrick Roy) were pushing goalies to be enormous walls of padding—not lithe acrobats
like Grant.

Grant:
When I started in Edmonton it was athletic. We moved around a lot,
because the game moved around a lot. Then it became very positional,
where everything taught was about angles, taking away space. It wasn't
so much you had to go get the puck—you just took away space and let
the puck come to you.

The change in equipment started with goalies such as Rejean
Lemelin going to new, lighter Aeroflex leg pads. They were cut
square and filled with foam instead of horsehair, and their
weight was almost half that of the old pads. What at first seemed
strange and uncomfortable soon became the standard for young
goalies entering the league, and the classic leather pads van-
ished within a few years. Similar innovations in gloves and body
armour followed.

Grant:

You couldn't go on with less equipment and guys shooting the puck at the same speed. That leaves marks, so the changes were good in that respect. But I really didn't go for the full switch. The new pads they wore kind of kicked out the puck. I wanted the puck to stay near; I didn't want it jumping all over the place. I tried some of the different pads over the years and didn't like the control they gave me, so I had a combination of the old and the new stuffing. It's the same with gloves: I always wore a small catcher's glove all the way right through to the end, just because I wanted to catch the puck and be able to control it. If the glove is too big you lose touch with the puck. Knocking it down doesn't do you any good; it means you've got to be able to find a rebound somewhere. By the time I retired, I was getting too old to try and chase it around, so you wanted to control it.

I was always taught that you're in control if you can catch the puck. You make it easier on your defencemen, more than anything.

The other innovation changing the sport was the use of video to analyze the tendencies and strategies of opponents. Roger Neilson—who coached seven different NHL teams—was the pioneer in the use of tape. Instead of coaches relying on their gut, they were now checking the video in between periods to improve their team. That also meant analyzing goalies such as Grant for ideas on where to shoot and how to distract him.

One of the major distractions for Grant the year before, of course, had been Kypreos. But this time there would be no Nick Kypreos to haunt him in the playoffs. Grant would get to start all of the Blues' games. Unfortunately, there wouldn't be that many of them. The first, however, was stellar: a shutout that stunned a Detroit crowd expecting their Red Wings to roll over the inferior Blues. Detroit outshot St. Louis 30–27 in that opening game, but they couldn't make a dent in Grant's defence. In the third period alone he turned aside 15 shots, including a full short-handed situation with two minutes to end the game. Detroit goalie Mike Vernon kept the game close, but he wasn't able to keep the Blues off the scoresheet.

Said Blues coach Joel Quenneville, after coaching his first NHL playoff game, "[Grant] made a couple of saves that were unbelievable. I don't know how he did that." Grant was more matter-of-fact. "Defence wins playoff games," he said. "We're playing good defense right now."

Grant's second shutout of the series was a 4–0 win at home in Game 4, which knotted the series at 2–2. Grant stopped all 28 shots from the powerful Red Wings offence led by Steve Yzerman, Sergei Fedorov and Brendan Shanahan. This was no ordinary Detroit team; it was a club embarking on the first of two straight Stanley Cups. So while Detroit rallied to win the next two games (and the series), Grant's play against the eventual champions was yet another example of how, even at age 35, he was still a goalie who saved his best for the big games. He posted a sparkling .929 save percentage in the series and a 2.18 GAA while recording two of his six career playoff shutouts. The Blues' inability to score on Detroit doomed the team—and Keenan. Now the only opponent who could get the best of Grant was Father Time.

GAME 10

y the time the St. Louis Blues headed into the 1999 Stanley Cup playoffs as the fifth seed in the Western Conference, financial pressures and the aging of an expensive roster were creating some uncomfortable choices. The showdown with Phoenix was looking like a last stand for many. For Grant, who'd been a bulwark for the Blues since 1995, that meant prospect Jamie McLennan was lurking on the horizon to play netminder for the Blues. Thanks to Grant's salary, the goalie position was one prominent place to make savings. Any kind of playoff disappointment that spring was going to make punting the future Hall of Famer to the curb easier to explain to Blues fans.

Things couldn't have started worse. Keith Tkachuk and the Coyotes jumped out to a quick 3–1 lead in the first-round playoff series. Grant was less than impressive as the Coyotes put 12 goals past him in those first four disheartening games. To coach Jim Schoenfeld's players, the Blues goalie seemed to have mentally checked out on the season. The Coyotes had heard stories that Grant was out playing golf—up to 36 holes—on his off days in the series. "We kept hearing these stories that he was playing golf instead of practising," says Laurence Gilman, then the assistant general manager in Phoenix. "Even allowing for Grant, that gave us some confidence."

It was just a matter of the Coyotes showing up for Game 5, claiming an easy victory on home ice and moving on. But Grant would once again remind the NHL that there was still a highly competitive player—even at the age of 36—in the St. Louis net. Led by his revived goaltending, the Blues clawed their way back into the series, tying it at three games apiece with an overtime victory in Game 5 followed by an emotional 5–3 win before the home fans at the Kiel Center. The 31-save performance forced a seventh game in Phoenix.

While the Coyotes geared for all hands on board in Game 7, some of the Blues players were worried about Grant's preparation. "The biggest thing Phoenix had was that white-out fan thing where everyone had white towels and it really pumped up their team," recalls Geoff Courtnall. "It was pretty intimidating going in there, and friggin' Fuhrsie is playing golf each day between our games. I was always worried about that; he's not practising. He's out playing 18 holes of golf; he's not resting between. How much is that going to cost us? But that's Fuhrsie. He wasn't worried about what he had to do, and he just came out there and stoned them. They didn't get a sniff. He's legendary."

Speaking of legends, Fuhr was playing golf with one while his teammates fretted.

Grant:

The day before Game 7 I played with Phil Mickelson in Phoenix. But that was my way of relaxing. I did the same thing when I was in Edmonton. It was Game 7; there wasn't much you could do but relax. I wasn't worried about what they were thinking. All I know is, it's been a good series the whole way through, we have as good a chance as they do, and all the pressure was on them—it's in their building. I knew from our Game 7 in Edmonton against Philadelphia in 1987, there's always more pressure on the home team. So I did what I normally do during the playoffs: just relax, go play golf, and you have a clear head going into the game.

The stage was set for Game 7. Coyotes star Jeremy Roenick, who'd missed the beginning of the series with a broken jaw, made it back into the Phoenix lineup. The Blues conscripted their walking wounded, too. Perhaps because it played out in a non-traditional hockey market, between two expansion teams, this Game 7 has not received the credit it is due. It was a classic, and the players and fans who were there that day will never forget it. For almost 78 minutes in the heat of a white-out Phoenix crowd (a tradition borrowed from the franchise's days in Winnipeg), Grant and Coyotes goalie Nikolai Khabibulin matched saves and kept the scoresheet blank. Blues defenceman Chris Pronger would log over 46 minutes while fellow defenceman Al MacInnis played 40. With shifts down to 30 seconds and lactic acid building in the legs of every skater, it seemed as though no one would ever score again.

Grant:

It was fun. Anytime you go into a Game 7 with Phoenix, they have the white out going, and a full house. I think they thought they were going to win. It had been a pretty offensive series, and you knew it was going to come down to who could make the last save. I found it relaxing that night: it was just one of those games where you feel comfortable right from the start. We got a couple lucky breaks along the way—I had one trickle through me that Jamie Rivers managed to grab just before the line. We just had a good feeling that it was our time to win.

Grant's instincts were accurate. With just over two minutes left in the first overtime period, a desperate Blues centre Pierre Turgeon reached out his stick to deflect a shot in mid-air from defenceman Ricard Persson. Khabibulin, who had been bracing himself for Persson's initial shot, was caught moving the wrong way. The puck flew by the startled Coyotes goalie into the net, and the rabid Phoenix crowd was struck dumb. Turgeon's desperate re-direct had clinched a 1–0 classic win for Joel Quenneville's squad. "They've got a very physical lineup, and we paid the price to win, but we came out of it alright," MacInnis told reporters afterwards.

The goalie who wouldn't go away suddenly looked like he was going to be in St. Louis a little while longer—at least into the next round against the powerful Dallas Stars. The revival pleased many in the hockey community. "(Fuhr) has been a treat to watch," said Toronto coach Pat Quinn. "He's one of those guys you hope never retires."

Grant:

Game 7; great hockey game. Not many Game 7s end up 1–0 in overtime. We were pretty happy about that. I was pretty happy. More playoff hockey. This time against Hully and Dallas.

The Dallas Stars, however, were well rested after eliminating Edmonton in a sweep, and many saw Bob Gainey's team as a potential Cup winner. They showed their form early as the Blues again fell behind in a series, this time two games to none. Again the Blues rallied at home, tying the series at two games each in front of enthusiastic fans at the Kiel Center. As the clubs headed back to Reunion Arena in Dallas, St. Louis was hoping for fate to repeat itself. Against the Coyotes, a Game 5 win on visitor's ice had been the springboard for the Blues to win the series. Could Grant make it happen again?

This time, however, there were no more miracles in the catching glove of a weary Grant Fuhr. The Stars' Ed Belfour outplayed him as Dallas scored the first goal in every game of the series. Propelled by Hull, Joe Nieuwendyk and Derian Hatcher, the Stars won the next two games—including a heartbreaking 2–1 OT loss for the Blues in Game 6 on St. Louis ice. Grant stopped 27 of 29 shots in his duel with Belfour, pushing the game into extra time. But Mike Modano's sudden-death goal sealed the series for the Stars, who went on to win the Cup. As well as he'd played for the Blues that post-season, Grant was left with a hollow feeling in the end.

Grant:

We beat good teams that spring. Then you end up losing, and you hate losing. We got used to winning here. It's in your blood that way. So it becomes frustrating. But at the same time you know you have a group that could win the next year. It's frustrating for a month or two and then all of a sudden training camp's there, and you're ready to go again.

As the teams shook hands at the conclusion of the series, Grant's outstanding performance had muddied the waters for the Blues' goaltending decisions. But once the emotions of the playoffs waned, it became clear that the Game 6 loss to Dallas would be Grant's last game in St. Louis and, ultimately, the final playoff game in his storied career. After the six wins in the 1999 post-season, his 92 playoff wins ranked him second all-time to Patrick Roy. (He's since been passed by Martin Brodeur, but Grant is unlikely to be threatened again anytime soon; Marc-Andre Fleury leads the active goalie club with 59 victories.)

After the season, the Blues opted not to re-sign the 36-year-old, banking on a tandem of McLennan and Czech prospect Roman Turek, acquired from Dallas (that duo would claim the Jennings Trophy a year later). Grant, meanwhile, was a free agent for the second time. While many wondered if this would be the end of his great career, one former rival thought there might be a last hurrah in the veteran. Brian Sutter had played for the Blues against Grant when he was on the triumphant Oilers, and had coached against Grant's Sabres when Buffalo upended Sutter's highly ranked Bruins in 1993.

Grant:

The last year I thought maybe I'd retire in St. Louis. We were looking at staying there and calling it a day. I'm a boring old guy at this point who likes to be in bed at 10:00, because the miles were ticking off quickly. But Brian Sutter had called St. Louis, and thought maybe it'd be nice if I could come to Calgary. Which, I have to admit, I had reservations about at the beginning. We didn't know how much we had in the tank left or where we were at.

By 2000, the once-proud Flames were in the midst of seven straight seasons outside the playoffs. The Canadian dollar was also plummeting, and ownership made no secret of needing the playoff revenue. With crowds dwindling at the Saddledome, the Flames needed some name recognition to harken back to the glory days of the Battle of Alberta. If Fuhr could play 50 games and help the Flames squeeze into a post-season berth, it would go a long way to help the franchise. So GM Al Coates and coach Sutter—whose jobs were clearly on the line—decided it was worth the risk.

Grant:

When I started the conversations with Brian, I was coming to Calgary
to play as a starter. That's why I left Los Angeles to go to St. Louis—so that
I could play. I couldn't just sit on the bench. I was never a guy who could
play once in awhile. There's no sense giving up on that part.

I knew all the Sutters. I played against Brian when he was in St. Louis.
I played against Brent and Darryl when they were with the Islanders. The
twins Rich and Ron were in Lethbridge when I played junior. I'd also been
at their different events in the summers and stuff in Alberta, but it was the
first time I played for one of them.

Being in Calgary would also bring Grant closer to his mother,
Betty, who'd been ill for some time.

Grant:

She'd been sick off and on for three or four years. She had three different
bouts of cancer, but the last year she was having a tough go of it. I'd been
through that with my dad, in terms of the cancer. His was quick, though.
Mom's was long and drawn out. I spent a lot of time on [Alberta] Highway 2
going back and forth between Edmonton and Calgary.

She'd never really given me heck about the crazy stuff I did, but
you could always tell that she wasn't impressed. There were brief
conversations. Then you'd get the, "You should probably be smart
now." Standard issue.

She was in her early 70s when I made it back to Calgary. I spent a lot
of time after practice driving to see her in Edmonton. I'd visit with her and
then drive all the way back down, go to practice the next day. We covered
a lot of miles. I talked to her every day. She was doing okay at that time.
It was more the last six or so months that she started to go downhill. She
was on and off at times.

And so Grant hauled his body to an NHL training camp for the final time. The changes in conditioning brought on by Bobby Kersee had helped him prolong his career. But there was only so much he could do at this point to stave off the inevitable.

Grant:

It was interesting to put on that Calgary jersey after all those years. I got a lot of heckling from friends up in Edmonton. But my mom was from Calgary, so it was okay to be a Flame. My old teammate Steve Smith had already been there for awhile—so it wasn't as big of a deal as it probably would have been earlier. Ten years previously? Not the same.

So I signed in September and headed to camp. That didn't feel too bad, but I also knew that wear and tear was catching up. I played a fair amount at the start of the year, but then the knee just got to a point where it wouldn't function anymore. The last year I played was a hard year. I mean, after about the first 10 games, the knee was just sore every day. I spent more time with [physical therapist] Terry Kane in the training room than I did on the ice, so the writing was on the wall at that point. I was always in an ice tub, trying to get the swelling to come out of the knee. That took the fun out of it.

But going to the rink was easy: Brian was fun to play for. Yeah, he screamed and yelled a little bit and you got mad. But it's no great secret. You put your time in with Brian and do what you're supposed to do; you never had an issue with him. We had some good guys on that team, like Jarome Iginla, that were good players and were going to beat you. The only guys that ran into an issue were the guys that didn't want to work 110 percent every day.

Grant was paired with backup goalie Fred Brathwaite, which meant that the Flames had two black goalies at the same time, an unprecedented situation for a full season in NHL history. As always

for Grant, the camaraderie of the dressing room was more important than the symbolism of his race. And that camaraderie included
mentoring the five-foot-nine Brathwaite.

Grant:

Freddy was a great roommate. I don't know how much I helped him, but
I had a lot of time for him. He never really got a chance to play in the NHL.
So that was a little unfortunate. I think Freddy had more talent than people
realized, but people at that time wanted big goalies. Everybody thinks you
have to be a great big guy to play goalie. They didn't think Fred was big
enough. I don't think size has anything to do with it. Bernie Parent was
not very big, but he was good. I'm not very big. I'm okay. Johnny Bower's
not very big. He was okay. Terry Sawchuk wasn't a great big man. He was
okay. Ken Dryden was the first successful big goalie. He was six foot four,
but he was athletic. I think you have to be mobile whether you're a big guy
like Ken or my size.

Watching the younger man starting out while his own career
was winding down, Grant could appreciate how far the sport had
come since the 1981–82 season when he'd broken in as the first
black goalie in league history.

Grant:

Hopefully you leave the game a little better than you got into it. I never
thought it was as big a deal as other people did. It means a lot more now,
a sense of your legacy. When you sit and think about it and you look at the
evolution of the game, I'm fortunate. I've become friends with Willie O'Ree,
who started it all for us back in 1958. When I was playing I got a chance
to meet Pokey Reddick, Mike Marson, Bill Riley, Tony McKegney, Claude
Vilgrain—guys like that. I'd always thought that was pretty cool.

For Jarome Iginla, the experience of playing with a role model was special: "I was a big fan of Grant Fuhr. I was a big Oilers fan growing up. I started out playing goal, but there wasn't enough action." Because Grant was a goalie, whose face was covered, many thought Iginla was the leader in the fight for recognition of visible minorities in hockey. "I was always the only black kid on my team and [sometimes] I'd get questions from my friends when I'd say, 'I want to be in the NHL,' and they'd say, 'Well, there are no black people or not very many in the NHL,' and as a kid, you'd wonder why. I think it'd be great to be a role model to kids. If a young black player can look at me and say, 'He did it, so I can, too,' I think that's fantastic. But I hope any young player can do the same."

Though the locker room camaraderie was good, things were diffi-cult for Grant on the ice. Plagued by his sore knees and shoulders, Grant played just 23 games in a campaign that would see both Coates and Sutter let go at season's end. Brathwaite took up the slack, posting five shutouts and a 2.75 GAA. By early April, with the Flames no longer in the playoff hunt, Grant confirmed the inevitable. Late in the season, after his old Blues team had elimi-nated the Flames' playoff hopes, he told reporters for the second time in his career that he was calling it quits. But this was no con-tract stunt—this time he meant it. "It's time," he told reporters. "The body says this is it."

Grant:

When you spend more time in the training room than you do on the ice, your number is close. I never wanted to be a backup, so it was time.
I was fortunate to play on good teams. Fortunate enough to enjoy the playoffs and know that it's the one thing that matters: winning. It still

goes back to that theory; contracts are great and everything if we want to go by numbers . . . but then you get to the playoffs and get swept in four games. I'd rather have bad numbers and then sweep somebody in four games. At the end of the day, it's win or lose, and I'll take winning every time. It would have been nice to win a Stanley Cup in another city, too—it would have been nice to add three or four more Cups. But we were fortunate enough to win five in Edmonton. You can't really be greedy and ask for more. It's a hard trophy to win once, and it's an even harder one to repeat. Look at Gretz—as great as he was, he didn't win any more Stanley Cups either. When the greatest player ever can't do it, it shows how hard it is.

On September 6, 2000, Grant made his retirement official at a press conference in Calgary, stating he could no longer risk irreparable damage to the knee that had troubled him since his run-in with Nick Kypreos in 1996 (he'd had three knee operations in two seasons, including one in March of 2000). "There is nothing like playing this great game, but the body is telling me it's time," Fuhr said at the Saddledome presser. "I leave the game knowing that it is the right decision and without any regrets. I will always treasure my time in the National Hockey League. I'm grateful to have played with some great players and some very successful teams."

As always, Grant was most proud of his winning record. He had rarely put much stock in the new statistical analysis that was overtaking hockey: his focus had been on when he made the saves, not how many he made. He would never claim many of the NHL's career statistical records for save percentage, GAA or shutouts—but his true impact is there in the win totals, especially in the postseason. At the time of his retirement announcement, his 403 wins were sixth most all-time, behind only Terry Sawchuk, Jacques Plante, Patrick Roy, Tony Esposito and Glenn Hall. (Martin Brodeur,

Patrick Roy and Ed Belfour have subsequently passed them all.) The only active goalie with a realistic chance of catching Grant for career wins in the near future is Roberto Luongo (with 373 wins through the 2013–14 season).

Grant's 868 games played, and a further 150 in the post-season—many on bad knees and with sore shoulders—are a testament to one of the most durable and reliable goalies in NHL history. "Grant was a true champion and one of the best goaltenders to ever play the game of hockey," recalls Mike Keenan, who saw many of Fuhr's best games in St. Louis and with Team Canada.

Grant also posted an eclectic resumé of NHL records: he holds the record for longest undefeated streak by a goaltender in his first NHL season (23 in 1981–82), the record for most assists in a single season by a goaltender (14 in 1983–84), the record for most games played by a goaltender in a single season (79 in 1995–96), and the record for most consecutive appearances in a single season by a goaltender (76 in 1996). He holds the NHL record in the current playoff format for greatest win percentage in a single post-season (a 16–2, .888 win percentage in 1988).

Grant's statistical impact is handicapped by the elimination of the NHL's tie rule in 2005 in favour of the shootout. Even a 50/50 split of the 114 ties in his career would have vaulted him to over 450 wins (and it's not hard to see how it might have been closer to 75 percent, given the mighty Oilers and their OT record.)

Grant:

I would have liked to have played a thousand games. We were close to that. Getting 400 wins was a goal: I got there. Four hundred and fifty was the actual goal: I didn't quite get there . . . a little shy of that. If we'd had the overtime shootout it might have been a few more losses, but it might have been a few more wins too. We might have got to 450 that way.

Like all retired players, Grant now faced the inevitable transition to normal life. Having watched as many of his friends went through the same process didn't make it any better. It's never an easy phase— even for those players who made millions in their careers. Few are completely ready for the lack of structure, the loss of hockey's highs and lows and the absence of dressing room camaraderie. For Grant, luckily, there remained a chance to stay in the game at the highest level. The Flames new general manager, Craig Button, offered him a goaltending consultant's job to help the transition and to mentor Brathwaite, a position he held for two seasons.

Grant:

The first couple of weeks after retiring were tough. You're up in the morning figuring you should be somewhere, and you've got nowhere to go. I was fortunate enough that I got to work for the Flames for a little bit as a consultant afterwards, so I still had somewhere to go. That never really transitioned completely, so I left Calgary and went back up to Edmonton for a year. Roamed around, coached my old junior team, the Cougars [now in Prince George, B.C.], and played golf for a year. Then I got the offer in 2004 from my old agent Mike Barnett to go down to Phoenix. He was running the Coyotes, and Gretz was a part owner. [Wayne would become coach in 2005.] Mike asked me if I'd like to go down there to coach the goalies. Hockey and golf; nothing wrong with that. I ended up in Phoenix for the next six years.

I enjoyed coaching. It's also frustrating, because you don't control what happens once they take the ice. You can only guide them to a certain point. Then it's out of your hands. Having played at an elite level, your instincts are maybe not their instincts. You can see it, but they may not see it that way. You'll find that a little bit frustrating.

But I was lucky enough to have good kids to work with. The first years I was there I had Brian Boucher, David Aebischer and Mikael Tellqvist.

We tried to do it by committee. They all were great No. 2 goalies, but nobody had been a No. 1 before. Then Curtis Joseph came in—a real pro—but we didn't get much better. In 2007 we brought in Ilya Bryzgalov. He'd won the Stanley Cup in Anaheim, but they had signed J.S. Giguere to a long deal. So there was no more room for [Ilya] with the Ducks, and we were able to get him on waivers. Brizzy was a different individual. He's the most talented goalie you'll ever see. If he really wants to, he can be as good as any in the game. He's got all the skills, all the talent. Just sometimes the focus was blurred a little bit.

Grant's work with the young goalies in San Antonio, Texas (the AHL affiliate at the time), impressed those around the Coyotes. Laurence Gilman, who was responsible for the Coyotes' farm system till 2007, marvelled at Grant's common touch. "Here was a guy who was a legend, larger-than-life for some of the young goalies we had in the system," Gilman recalls. "He could have made himself remote and unapproachable. But he had such a common, unassuming attitude with the young guys. Despite all his accomplishments, he treated them as if he were just another ordinary guy. That always impressed me: just how down-to-earth he was, always looking to help."

Phoenix was also an opportunity to again catch up with Wayne Gretzky as the Great One launched his coaching career. Although he had no experience as a head coach, he took over from Rick Bowness in an attempt to jump-start a winning tradition in the desert and—if that failed—at least draw the curious to the rink to see him behind the bench.

Grant:
It was fun to watch Gretz coach. Ultra competitive. You're sitting in the coach's room, you get to hear some of his theories on playing. His dad,

Walter, had been ahead of his time in how he'd coached Wayne, and I think Wayne wanted to put the same sort of practices to work for himself. I think he got a little frustrated sometimes, because things that he saw that were simple and understood, some of the guys had a hard time picking up.

In exhibition games you'd see a lot of the kids looking behind the bench while a game's going on. They couldn't help it. You get to see the greatest player in the game, he's standing up behind you, and you're looking to see what he's doing. If you're 18, 19 years old, it's just an instinct. If I was an 18-year-old kid sitting there, I'd be looking back to see what's going on.

It was hard on Gretz. Unfortunately, we didn't have the success that we should have had. We had some teams that were good teams, but they just ran out of steam because we were too young. Usually about mid-February, late March, we would lose eight or nine games in a row, and all of a sudden you're out the playoffs. You could have three-quarters of a good year, then that last quarter would bite you. We had that happen about three years in a row, where we'd have a little stretch of two or three weeks where we wouldn't play well. Unfortunately, in the Western Conference you can't have two or three weeks where you don't play well. And it didn't help the fans coming, either: everybody wants to see a winner, and if you're not winning in Phoenix there's other things [for the fans] to see and do.

As the club's failures accumulated, critics began to suggest that perhaps the tolerance level for the mistakes of young players was not as high as it should have been. On the other hand, Gretzky and Fuhr were trying to teach accountability on the ice. Given the numerous other distractions, especially the club's precarious financial situation, they tried to control the thing they could control— the team's play.

Grant:

Especially toward the end, who knew when the next cheque was coming? You could get sidetracked by that. We tried not to worry about that as coaches. That's the business side of hockey. As a player or coach, that's not really your biggest concern. Your biggest concern is trying to be successful on the ice.

I'm sure it bothered some of the players, but we just tried to instill in them that all of that stuff is out of your hands anyway. It's easy to cloud your head with six thousand different things, but if you've got one task that you actually control, it's a lot easier to control one task. That was something I could always do, concentrate on one thing at a time.

Making it even harder to keep young players' minds on the task at hand, Grant believed, was the evolving contract climate produced by new collective bargaining agreements in 1995 and 2005. Salaries touched the $10-million-a-year mark. Players as young as their early 20s were suddenly making five or six million dollars a year on five- or six-year guaranteed contracts. One good year could make you rich for life, and because of that, winning itself was not always the priority: numbers were. Suddenly, players didn't always want a role that might guarantee wins for the team but wouldn't guarantee them the individual numbers they coveted.

In the end, the Coyotes made the playoffs only once in the years Grant and Gretz were reunited in Phoenix, and failures on the ice produced big losses at the box office. Before the NHL finally took over in 2009, chaos reigned in the front office. In May of 2007, Mike Barnett and his management team of Cliff Fletcher and Laurence Gilman were fired, and Don Maloney was hired to run the team. The new management wanted a different voice for the goalies, so Grant was made director of goalie development with Sean Burke taking over as goalie coach. Grant remained in the position for a year before deciding he liked the hands-on experience better.

Grant:

I went back to Edmonton for a year and coached minor hockey—which I truly enjoyed. Some of the parents were a little off the wall, but the teaching was enjoyable. I think there's a real need for coaching goalies at the grassroots level in Canada: over the years, goalies have always been overlooked. It's an important position where, for the longest time, everybody seemed to assume that Canadian goalies were good—and for the longest time they were. Now, everybody else has developed their goalies more, especially Europe in recent years. American goalies seem to be the hot item right now.

Over the last few years the Canadians have basically said, "He's our guy," without having played games or exhibitions or anything. I think it takes the competitive fire out of it. I'd rather see a camp where you go in and nobody knows whether they're going to be the guy or not. They're in it to play.

After a year in Edmonton, golf came hunting for Grant. The Canadian owners of Desert Dunes in Palm Springs, California, were looking for a name to attract the snowbirds to their Robert Trent Jones layout. And Grant was looking for an entree into the golf business. In 2013, he was hired as director of golf at the club.

Grant:

Since I've retired, I think I've only spent maybe two years out of the eight away from the NHL. One of the years I spent out of the game, I coached minor hockey in Edmonton. So I've never really been away, away. But I also wanted to play some serious golf, and now I get the opportunity to work at Desert Dunes and learn some new things about running a golf course.

We're now learning the golf business from scratch. I find it interesting; at the same time it's occasionally overwhelming. The guys I work with here, they go to school for turf care or pro shop management—they've studied for it. I've gotten to know some really good people here at Desert Dunes. Our superintendent is fabulous, and I've gotten to know some of the other superintendents. I got to know some of the directors of golf here in Palm Springs. I know a bunch of the tour pros, and I know people in the different equipment companies. Myself, I just go by what would I like in a golf club.

While he may be new to the business of golf, Grant has long been teeing it up with top players such as Phil Mickelson, and fellow Canadian Mike Weir.

Grant:
Phil was fun to play with, just to see what he could do with the golf ball. You realize he's good from watching on TV and everything, but then you get to see it first-hand and it's so good. So much fun to watch. Mike Weir. He turned out pretty good, didn't he? Won a Masters and such. I met him when he played the Canadian Tour. Even when they're not grinding or competing, you see how good they are.

Grant also played the celebrity golf circuit for retired athletes. He tied for third in both the 2007 and 2008 American Century Celebrity Golf championships, including five top-six finishes in the past nine years. As a result, he now counts dozens of actors, former athletes and celebrities as friends. On any given day he might be teeing it up with actor Bill Murray, NFL legends Jim McMahon, Marshall Faulk, Emmitt Smith and Tony Romo or NBA Hall of Famer Charles Barkley.

Grant:

I was with Mac [McMahon] and Charles [Barkley] for New Year's. Charles has a party every year, so I go over to see Charles. He is awesome. Really good person. I'm a better golfer than Charles; I know that. But he's a lot of fun to be around. The actor Jack Wagner and I played a bunch when I was in L.A. It was me, him and Danny Quinn, who played for Pittsburgh and L.A. in the NHL. We played a lot of golf together. Who else did I play with? Brian Baumgartner, from *The Office*. He's a lot of fun. Had a good time playing with him. We have become good friends.

No mystery there. By the time the Hall of Fame called, it was safe to say everyone was friends with Grant Fuhr.

EXTRO

The lights may be down at Edmonton's Skyreach Centre on the night of October 10, 2003, but everyone is home. The Oilers are opening their season against the San Jose Sharks, but that's only one part of the celebration for the fans turning out on this autumn evening. The city of Edmonton has come to honour the guy from Spruce Grove who, with his brilliant goaltending, helped turn their team into a five-time champion, perhaps the final NHL dynasty before salary caps ruined the concept.

At the entrance to the ice, an enormous cloud of dry ice vapour is whipped up, and lights catch what looks to be the shape of a goalie. The crowd goes wild. Suddenly a spotlight switches to the far end of the rink. There is a familiar shape standing in the blue paint of the Oilers goal. Longtime Edmonton fans recognize the goaltender's equipment of a bygone era, the iconic white Edmonton Oilers jersey from the glory years of 1980–1990, the mask with its orange and blue stripes. The mysterious figure's nervous shifting from one skate to the other is another flashback to the days when this team's goalie was the NHL's supreme closer. The crowd pours out its heart to the agile man between the pipes.

Grant:

You're there in the dark, and you can hear the noise of the crowd, and you know what's going to happen because they've scripted it for weeks. You're prepared for it. I'd seen Gretz's ceremony, I'd seen Mess's retirement ceremony . . . You get the gist as to what was going on. You've seen it in rehearsal. Looks very easy: go there, stand there, move here . . . Until you step out—and then you actually see it. They forgot to mention it's a lot of people. It's a lot easier to be a spectator.

Grant Fuhr was always unconventional. Consider his acrobatic style, throwing himself recklessly across the crease; his "unique" approach to conditioning; his role as a pioneer in a sport long considered hostile to visible minorities; his documented personal issues while winning the Stanley Cup and Canada Cup at the peak of his career in the 1980s; his undying devotion to golf, a sport that, for most hockey fans, is just code for elimination from the playoffs.

So when the time came for the Oilers to honour him on the eve of his inclusion in the Hockey Hall of Fame, there would be no uncomfortable suit and tie at centre ice, no walking out nervously on the red carpet. There would be Grant, in his Oiler jersey once more, wearing his NHL equipment for the first time since his retirement and skating on the Northlands ice one last time for the fans. Let them see him as he was.

The PA booms: "Ladies and gentlemen, hockey fans, wearing his familiar No. 31, Grant Fuhr!" And with that, a spotlight finds Grant in his "office." The mask comes off to reveal the guest of honour, looking slightly taken aback by the fuss. Even today, seeing the black face behind the mask is a reminder of how far he has brought the sport in its acceptance of visible minorities. As the cheers wash down to ice level, Grant skates slowly through the dark, the wrap-around signage blaring "Grant Welcome Home." There is a wall of noise for the man who left Edmonton at his peak, but not of his own volition. For a time there was a distance between the player and the team as Grant suited up in five other NHL uniforms. But now he is home and getting the love of the people once more. He is the point of light in the darkened arena.

As he glides beside the boards, the familiar faces from Spruce Grove, from Edmonton and from his hockey life appear in the stands. While his parents, Bob and Betty, cannot be here (except in Grant's heart), his children and cousins and uncles and aunts dot the sellout crowd.

Grant:

Even in the dark I could see them from where I was. The lights are out, but you can actually see them. You recognize so many people—and that's overwhelming. Seeing people from all parts of my life there: friends from Spruce Grove, Edmonton, Calgary. That was fun. The speaking is not fun, but in a way, I do enjoy thanking those people who helped me. As you're standing there, you're in a mad panic thinking again about who you might have forgotten—you're trying to remember them all. I think that's the biggest fear. Forgetting somebody.

Having eschewed the tuxedo, there was the issue of how to represent Grant's long NHL career in five cities. Though the focus was unquestionably on the Oilers, the uniform for the evening had been carefully assembled from the equipment Grant had worn during his 17-year tenure in the NHL.

Grant:

It was the first time I'd put the equipment on since retiring. The Hall of Fame had sent my mask back to me for that night. We had the original.

The under-body stuff was from St. Louis. The gloves were from St. Louis. The pants were a pair that I had worn in Edmonton. Even the Brown neck protector. It was a mismatch of equipment. We were a little afraid it might not fit anymore, because I wasn't exactly slim at that point. But it worked out great.

I came to the arena that night and we were way over in one of the back dressing rooms, because the guys were getting ready to play—you don't want to be a distraction to them. I walked into that room, and the equipment's hanging there like it always did. Sparky's around there, Joey's around there. So you sit back there and have a couple of cold beverages beforehand to take the edge off.

Then you start to put the stuff on—it's like you go by memory and by Braille—what goes where again? That's the other hard part. I literally hadn't touched equipment since I retired. I swore I was never going to put it back on again. And it led to doing the Heritage Classic in Edmonton, and once a year doing Gretz's fantasy camp.

As the crowds cheer their hero, Grant struggles to sum up his feelings about the team he starred for, the people he played with and the times—both good and bad—that he'd seen in the Alberta capital. "I have been part of a lot of opening nights, but none better than this," he tells the crowd. "Everybody here stuck with me and that's a beautiful thing. The group of guys we had here were just one big family. I was happy to be a part of that."

Then, in his understated style, he allows for his nerves. "I hate speaking. I made more speeches in the last two days than I will make in the rest of my life." Then the jersey ascends to the rafters. As his eyes wells with tears, former teammate Kevin Lowe—then president and GM of the Oilers—brings him a bottle of water.

Grant:

It's a great honour to see your name go up there. But it's also fun to see the company it's up there with. You think: it was a pretty good hockey team. Some great friends and great players.

If there's one thing I want all those people to know it's that I enjoyed doing it every day more than anything. Loved the process of what it takes to play at this level. I might have done it a little differently than most people. I probably had more fun than I should have, but I enjoyed every minute of it.

ACKNOWLEDGMENTS

I have a lot of people to thank for making this book possible so here it goes.

First and foremost, I want to thank my parents for making me the person I am and for the chance to grow up and be successful at what I wanted to be; for their belief in me, and for making it all possible through their own sacrifice. Second of all, my kids, for it is you who made a huge sacrifice by me not being there as much as you would have liked—and for the time that we missed that every parent should have with their children. Next I want to thank all the management, players and coaches I've had. You are as close to family as it gets without being family, and I owe a lot of the person I am to your love and support. I want to thank one of my best friends and my accountant, Brian Farrell: you have been with me through thick and thin, and it is with your help that I have learned the harder parts of life. Barry Rimmer has been my best friend every step of the way, and everyone should be so lucky as to have a best friend like this. I don't even know how to thank you enough—you have been the one rock in my life. I want to thank all my aunts and uncles as well: I could not have been adopted into a better family. To my lovely wife-to-be Lisa Cavanaugh, thank you, as it's been your love and support that has allowed me to comfortable enough in my own skin to finish this book. You loved me as a person before you ever had any idea what I ever did in life. Lastly I want to thank all my fans, for it is you who allowed me to live my dream, and supported me through good, bad and ugly.

I am truly the luckiest man in the world to have had so much love and support. Thank you all from the bottom of my heart.

Bruce Dowbiggin

Thank you to Paul Taunton for his vigilant editing on the manuscript and Linda Pruessen for the copy edit. Thanks to Evan Dowbiggin for his excellent research and fact checking.

I would like to thank his agent Jake Elwell of Harold Ober Associates for his diligent work in bringing the project to life over several years of hard work. As always, thanks to Meredith, Evan, Rhys and Clare for their support.

SELECTED REFERENCES

Chaput, John. "Shupe Unhappy Fuhr's Practice Makes Near-Perfect." *Canadian Press*, December 20, 1980.

"Cougars Continue Comeback But It's No Surprise to Them." *Canadian Press*, May 1, 1981.

DelNagro, Mike. "The Lord of the Rinks." *Sports Illustrated*, February 15, 1982.

Dowbiggin, Bruce. *Of Ice and Men: The Craft of Hockey*. Toronto: Macfarlane Walter & Ross, 1998.

Dryden, Ken. *The Game*. Toronto: John Wiley & Sons, 1983.

Elliott, Helene. "His Career Was Saved by Leaving the Kings." *Los Angeles Times*, December 10, 1995.

Falla, Jack. "The Oilers Were the Spoilers." *Sports Illustrated*, May 28, 1984.

"Fuhr Tries to Pick Up Pieces." *Edmonton Sun*, October 1, 1990.

Greenberg, Jay. "A Happy Return Goalie Grant Fuhr Picks Up Where He Left Off." *Sports Illustrated*, March 4, 1991.

Gzowski, Peter. *The Game of Our Lives*. Toronto: McClelland & Stewart, 1982.

Hunt, Jim. *The Men in the Nets*. Chicago: Follett Publishing Company, 1967.

Johnson, George. "Fuhr's Career Concern: Winning." ESPN.com, November 3, 2003, http://sports.espn.go.com/nhl/columns/story?id=1650401.

Kelley, Jim. "Fuhr Not Ready to Concede Starting Job." *Buffalo News*, March 23, 1994.

Keteyian, Armen. "The Joyless End to a Joyride." *Sports Illustrated*, May 12, 1986.

McMillan, Tom. "Gretzky Leads Canada to Tie with Soviets."
    Pittsburgh Post-Gazette, September 7, 1987.

Murphy, Austin. "Old Faithful." *Sports Illustrated*, February 19, 1996.

——. "Party Time in Edmonton." *Sports Illustrated*, June 8, 1987.

Panaccio, Tim. "Another Breakthrough for Grant Fuhr." *The
    Philadelphia Inquirer*, November 8, 2003.

Rosa, Francis. "Fuhr Is an Ace." *Boston Globe*, May 21, 1987.

——. "Fuhr the Next One to Be Fit for Kings?" *Boston Globe*,
    January 29, 1989.

Sassone, Tim. "Numerous NHL Camps Plagued by a Long List of
    Notable Absentees." *Daily Herald*, September 10, 1999.

Scher, Jon. "Twin Peaks." *Sports Illustrated*, May 5, 1993.

Taylor, Jim. http://www.drjimtaylor.com/3.0/consulting/prime-sport/.

"Tiger Goes Against the Grain." *Associated Press*, March 26, 2000.

Wiley, Ralph. "The Puck Stops Here." *Sports Illustrated*, January 11,
    1988.

Wolff, Jana. *Secret Thoughts of an Adoptive Mother*. Honolulu: Vista
    Communications, 2010.

INDEX

GRANT FUHR was the Hall of Fame goaltender for the Edmonton Oilers, and the first black superstar in the National Hockey League. He is now a role model and fundraiser for charity, inspiring young goalies around the world. Fuhr is a scratch golfer who participates in numerous celebrity golf events for charity throughout the year. He lives in Edmonton, Alberta.

BRUCE DOWBIGGIN has covered hockey for the CBC (where he won two Gemini awards as Canada's top sportscaster), the *Calgary Herald*, and *The Globe and Mail*; and is the author of several bestselling hockey books. He lives in Calgary, Alberta.